Cambridge Elements

MAKING CITIES SOCIALIST

Katherine Zubovich
University at Buffalo, SUNY

Shaftesbury Road, Cambridge CB2 8EA, United Kingdom

One Liberty Plaza, 20th Floor, New York, NY 10006, USA

477 Williamstown Road, Port Melbourne, VIC 3207, Australia

314–321, 3rd Floor, Plot 3, Splendor Forum, Jasola District Centre, New Delhi – 110025, India

103 Penang Road, #05–06/07, Visioncrest Commercial, Singapore 238467

Cambridge University Press is part of Cambridge University Press & Assessment, a department of the University of Cambridge.

We share the University's mission to contribute to society through the pursuit of education, learning and research at the highest international levels of excellence.

www.cambridge.org
Information on this title: www.cambridge.org/9781009468077

DOI: 10.1017/9781108850520

When citing this work, please include a reference to the DOI 10.1017/9781108850520

First published 2024

A catalogue record for this publication is available from the British Library.

ISBN 978-1-009-46807-7 Hardback
ISBN 978-1-108-79710-8 Paperback
ISSN 2632-3206 (online)
ISSN 2632-3192 (print)

Making Cities Socialist

Elements in Global Urban History

DOI: 10.1017/9781108850520
First published online: February 2024

Katherine Zubovich
University at Buffalo, SUNY

Author for correspondence: Katherine Zubovich, kzubovic@buffalo.edu

Abstract: This Element explores the history of urban planning, city building, and city life in the socialist world. It follows the global trajectories of architects, planners, and ideas about socialist urbanism developed during the twentieth century, while also highlighting features of everyday life in socialist cities. The Element opens with a section on the socialist city as it took shape first in the Soviet Union. Subsequent sections take a comparative and transnational approach to the history of socialist urbanism, tracing socialist city development in the Union of Soviet Socialist Republics (USSR), Eastern Europe, Asia, Africa, and Latin America.

Keywords: cities, socialism, urban, socialist, history

ISBNs: 9781009468077 (HB), 9781108797108 (PB), 9781108850520 (OC)
ISSNs: 2632-3206 (online), 2632-3192 (print)

Contents

1 Introduction

Broad paths cutting through the residential district made the new town of Cheremushki good for strolling, even on a cold winter day. The photograph in Figure 1 shows residents of this Soviet city out for a walk. Pushing their baby in a pram, with another child walking closely behind, the young family passes by birch trees, conifers, and a communal laundry line with sheets hung out to dry. A dozen or so prams belonging to other families living in the neighborhood are parked by each of the entrances to the apartment complex on the right. Benches near each entryway accommodate sitting outside when the weather warms. Another apartment building stands in the distance. This neighborhood, with its cluster of five-story buildings, was brand new, built for workers of the nearby Sayano-Shushenskaya dam located along the Yenisei River in southwestern Siberia. The first turbine of the dam, still one of the world's largest hydroelectric power plants today, whirled into action in 1978, one year after this photograph was taken. The dam was designed by engineers in Leningrad, some 5,000 kilometers away. And like its designers, the dam's workers also came from afar. It is likely that the residents pictured here were newcomers to this remote region, having joined thousands of other young workers like them in building and maintaining the dam and in populating this new Soviet town.

While residents of Cheremushki spent their days maintaining a unique piece of hydroelectric infrastructure, the urban settlement to which they returned each evening was not unique at all. Even the name of their new town signaled its ordinariness. Cheremushki (pronounced "cher-YO-moosh-ki," from the word "cheremukha" or bird cherry tree) was a common name for new towns and suburban districts in the Soviet Union. (The name was so common that the Cheremushki pictured in this photograph is not the only Cheremushki along the Yenisei River. A second one is located 350 kilometers north.) Specialist readers will know that the most famous Cheremushki in the USSR was in the Soviet capital city of Moscow. In the late 1950s, Moscow's Novye (New) Cheremushki district was the site of experiments in prefabricated mass housing construction. Ideas pioneered in Moscow in the 1950s can be seen in the Cheremushki along the Yenisei in the 1970s: the buildings in the photograph are similar to designs implemented in the southwest district of the capital two decades earlier.

There are distinctive features of the Cheremushki located along the Yenisei River, of course, like the dramatic peaks of the Sayan mountain range that frame the town before unfolding southward toward neighboring Mongolia. This corner of Siberia also has the distinction of being the site where a young revolutionary named Vladimir Ulyanov, who would soon adopt the pseudonym "Lenin," served time in exile after Russian Tsarist officials found him guilty of

Figure 1 Residents of Cheremushki, located near the Sayano-Shushenskaya hydro power station, USSR, 1977.

sedition in 1897. But aside from these unique geographical and historical features, most elements of this Cheremushki along the Yenisei would have felt wholly familiar to the neighborhood's inhabitants regardless of where in the Soviet Union they were from. Right down to the design of the benches by the entryways, the five-story prefabricated apartment blocks pictured here were ubiquitous in cities across the USSR and beyond by the 1970s. Isolated though they were in their remote new town, the family in this photograph lived in a socialist city that formed part of a global network of urban spaces, connected by a shared set of spatial and ideological practices.

1.1 What Makes a City "Socialist"?

In 1974, three years before the photograph in Figure 1 was taken, Henri Lefebvre posed the following question in his book *The Production of Space*: "Has state socialism produced a space of its own?" For Lefebvre, the answer was no. The French Marxist philosopher and urban thinker argued that "a social transformation, to be truly revolutionary in character, must manifest a creative capacity in its effects on daily life, on language and on space" (1974, 62). In comments that reflected in part his own disappointment with the course socialism had taken in the USSR, Lefebvre acknowledged that while there were inklings in the utopian 1920s of the emergence of a new, distinctly socialist space in the Soviet Union, the advent of Stalinism in 1928 had ensured that "those fertile years were followed by years of sterility." Writing at a time when a significant and growing proportion of the world was governed by state socialism, Lefebvre contentiously argued that no revolutionary social transformation had taken place under socialism and that, consequently, there was little difference between socialist and capitalist spaces. New political institutions and ideological superstructures may have been created in the Soviet Union and elsewhere, Lefebvre wrote, but "a revolution that does not produce a new space has not realized its full potential." "No architectural innovation has occurred, no specific space has been created," Lefebvre concluded.[1] For the French philosopher, there was no such thing as a "socialist city."

Lefebvre's assertion that state socialism failed to produce "a space of its own" has long been contradicted by researchers working across a variety of disciplines and geographies. Many of the French theorist's own contemporaries specializing in the study of state socialism not only stressed the differences that had emerged between capitalist and socialist cities, but also argued in favor of categorizing the socialist city as a distinct urban type. The 1970s saw large growth in the anglophone scholarship on socialist cities. British geographers R. A. French and F. E. Ian Hamilton's edited volume of 1979, *The Socialist City: Spatial Structure and Urban Policy*, brought together a range of experts working on cities in the USSR and Eastern Europe. French and Hamilton's pioneering volume covered topics from planning and decision-making to housing and urban recreational spaces. Sections highlighted the construction of new industrial cities while also examining how socialist architects and urban planners in historic cities like Moscow and Warsaw contended with the centuries-old urban fabric inherited from prerevolutionary years. The volume also discussed socialist mass housing, built from the late 1950s on the outskirts of existing cities and in remote resource-rich regions, which had created "a certain degree of uniformity in cities throughout the Soviet Union and Eastern Europe" (14). French and Hamilton argued that socialist cities differed from capitalist cities because of the high degree of state control under socialism over the economy, land use, industrialization, population movement, and myriad other factors. The abolition of private property and state ownership of the means of production gave socialist officials unparalleled control over decision-making. While not their focus, French and Hamilton might also have included new degrees of state control over urban expertise in their list of factors making socialist cities unique. The new schools and architectural academies established on the Soviet model in communist Eastern Europe after 1945 not only ensured greater state oversight

[1] On Henri Lefebvre's ideas about socialist space, see Stanek 2011.

of urban experts, but also served initially to Stalinize Eastern European architectural practice.

In the four to five decades since French and Hamilton published their book on socialist cities, there have been several twists and turns in the history of state socialism. There have also been significant developments in how scholars understand socialist urbanism. First, increased attention to spaces outside the USSR and Eastern Europe has enriched and refined our understanding of the complex relationship between cities and socialism. Not all socialist states were committed to the Soviet dictate that urbanism was a cornerstone of socialist life. In fact, some socialist states actively worked to curb urban growth, prioritizing rural and agricultural development instead. Examples include the outflow of China's urban youth to the countryside during the Cultural Revolution of 1966–1976 and Cuba's plan of the late 1960s to "urbanize the country and ruralize the city." The "ruralization" of cities in China and the "anti-urban" approach adopted in countries like Tanzania and Cuba were taken by some scholars as features of a new type of socialist city altogether (French and Hamilton 1979, 3; Forbes and Thrift 1987). Earlier scholarship tended to draw a line between socialist cities in Asia, Africa, and Latin America and those in Europe (a term that usually included the USSR, though of course the Soviet Union included vast territory encompassing parts of Europe and Asia). More recently, scholarship not only compares cities across different regions but also shows how socialist cities around the globe were connected in significant and lasting ways. As scholars have moved from comparative to more integrative approaches, research increasingly highlights the interlinkages between socialist cities – interlinkages that form the basis for what has been called "second world urbanity" (Zarecor 2018; Bocharnikova and Harris 2018) and "socialist world-making" (Stanek 2022).

Second, the scholarship on socialist cities has been shaped by the fall of communism in Eastern Europe in the late 1980s and the breakup of the Soviet Union in the early 1990s. This moment of rupture, now three decades in the past, opened to scholars of these regions new levels of access to archival documents and research sites. During what is often called the "archival revolution" of the 1990s, researchers of the former Soviet Union and Eastern Europe were granted new levels of access to historical materials and documents, a change that generated new research questions and new findings. At the same time, as political and economic transitions began in Eastern Europe and in the newly independent countries formed in the place of the former Soviet Union's fifteen titular republics, researchers began to scrutinize a new urban type: the post-socialist city. In the process of studying the effects of political and economic transition on cities *after* communism, scholars began to reassess and redefine the socialist city. A vast literature dealing with the socialist and post-socialist city in Eastern Europe emerged in the 1990s and early 2000s. With a wider range of research materials at their disposal and with an end point for socialist urbanism in view, it was possible to pin down a set of defining features for the socialist city, at least in its East European and Soviet variations.

In her scholarship on transformations to the built environment in post-socialist Sofia, Bulgaria, Sonia Hirt highlights the key features that made cities socialist, including a lack of suburban sprawl; an abundance of public buildings, parks, and plazas; a surfeit of consumer retail spaces; and a surplus of both industrial spaces and symbolic features including monuments and statuary. Compared to capitalist cities, socialist cities were denser, more compact, featured less urban informality, and tended to be less socially segregated. While capitalist cities developed in the twentieth century in response to growing rates of private car ownership, socialist city builders focused on developing robust public transit systems catering to a population without broad access to private vehicles (Hirt 2012, 35–37). Although the neoclassical design characteristic of Socialist Realism prevailed in earlier decades, by the 1960s, Hirt notes, socialist cities tended to be dominated by "an especially spartan branch of modernism," a feature that created a drab, gray, and boring appearance (2006, 36). Hirt also argues that socialist officials, architects, and urban planners were much more deliberate than their counterparts working in capitalist cities in approaching the built environment as a powerful tool of governance. As she writes, "shaping space to shape a new society was *the business* of the socialist state to a far greater extent than in capitalist nations" (2006, 37).

Housing and everyday life were a particular focus of socialist leaders, architects, and planners eager to shape the lives of residents through the reshaping of urban space. And this subject has necessarily garnered the attention of a wide range of scholars. In the Soviet Union, attending to the "housing question," as it was termed, enabled socialist leaders to extend their managerial oversight into the realm of everyday life – a concept that Deirdre Ruscitti Harshman notes was embraced early on by the Soviet state itself. "State-level institutions," she writes, "promoted the creation of a new everyday life (*novyi byt*)," a process that would be achieved through the work of neighborhood and local-level groups that "formed Cultural Everyday Life Institutions . . . involved in creating and running cafeterias, children's playgrounds, bathhouses, libraries, and more" (2018, 3). Located more often than not in urban spaces, such groups and the "everyday life" programs they managed helped to alleviate the stress of rapid urbanization and upheaval that characterized the first decades, at least, of socialism in the Soviet Union. As socialism spread to other parts of the world, the concern for housing and everyday life moved along with the politics.

Anthropologist Christina Schwenkel notes that scholars working on socialism in the post-1945 period have shown that "housing, in particular, embodied the hopeful promise of socialism, with the provision of separate family apartments serving as an instrumental means to produce a population trained in the socialist arts of modern living" (2020, 29). Socialist programs and strategies for attending to the everyday shifted over time and space. Socialist urbanites lived in a wide range of housing types, from communal apartments and barracks to tents and Chinese *gandalei* dry-pounded earth houses. In the 1950s, socialist single-family apartments were built in the Soviet Union and elsewhere in the socialist world on a mass scale using prefabricated technologies. The attention given to questions of residential and daily life was a feature of what made cities socialist. Yet, this is not to say that socialist planners were always, or often, successful in attending to the "housing question" and in managing everyday life in socialist cities. Scholarship abounds in examples of dashed hopes, crushed dreams, and failed urban projects. Shortages of consumer goods in many socialist cities made waiting in line a daily reality. Socialist cities could be spaces of intense social segregation, where elites guarded access to limited amenities and resources. New forms of surveillance and new types of disciplinary and carceral spaces also emerged in cities throughout the socialist world, creating tense dynamics between citizens and the state. Still, recent scholarship encourages us to move beyond these now familiar narratives of failure, reframing socialist cities not only as spaces where people lived rich and complex lives but also as spaces that continue to exist and shape the present, even in countries that have long been "post-socialist" (Murawski 2018).

Before the Second World War, socialist cities existed in the Soviet Union alone. But from years thereafter, this urban type spread as communism traveled to new parts of the world. By 1980, the socialist world encompassed large parts of Asia, Africa, and Europe, as well as areas of Latin America. Not only had state socialism produced "a space of its own," it had also generated widespread exchange between cities, leading to key similarities as well as differences across socialist locales in places as distant as Havana and Ulaanbaatar. Socialist cities share a common set of traits. Even so, what defined a socialist city changed dramatically over space and time. As socialism developed and spread during the twentieth century, socialist planning principles were applied in an increasingly diverse range of places, leading to innovations, differences, and greater variety. It is not unreasonable to question whether there ever was a "socialist city." This Element proceeds from the position that there was. But it is worth noting that the doubts expressed by Lefebvre worried socialist planners themselves long before the French theorist posed his provocative question in 1974.

1.2 Socialist Cities through Socialist Eyes

Whether socialism ever produced an urban space uniquely its own is a question that animated Soviet architects and urban planners in the 1920s and 1930s. Urban experts working in the world's first socialist state had no blueprint for how to make their cities socialist. Karl Marx and Friedrich Engels, who supplied the mid-nineteenth-century socialist movement with its most trenchant critiques of capitalism and its social consequences, had much to say about capitalist cities. Nineteenth-century industrial cities intensified the inequalities and contradictions of capitalism. Engels's *The Condition of the Working Class in England*, published in 1845 and based on the author's own observations of urban life in Manchester and London, described in ethnographic detail the squalid living and working conditions, environmental degradation, and spatial segregation that characterized early industrial cities. The view offered by Engels was in line with the observations of other social thinkers of the nineteenth and early twentieth centuries. And it was a view that the new Soviet Union's Bolshevik leaders had in mind when they set about making their cities socialist. As historian Glennys Young observes, questions of space and the built environment loomed large in communist thought. "As Marx and his followers divided human history into classes," Young writes, "they also divided it into different types of space. Feudal space, for example, was that of the aristocratic estate and the 'backward' peasant. The spaces of the bourgeoisie were the offices of high capital, the factories that caused workers to suffer immiseration and alienation, and the battlefields where the colonizers defeated the colonized" (2011, 230). The path toward socialism and then communism promised to transform space anew, reforming it to suit the newly ruling working class or proletariat. Factories, as Young writes, "would be transformed from sites of suffering to palaces of labor."

Still, communist thinkers offered no defined vision for the future of urbanism in socialism or communism. As Soviet state official Lazar Kaganovich put it, "Marx and Engels never attempted to define the definite social forms of the future communist society; on the contrary, they warned us against preoccupying ourselves with such matters. Their position was that the proletariat, after it had seized power, would step by step, in the very process of the socialist reconstruction of society, experience the need for, and create, each specific new form of life" (1931, 83). Ultimately, Marx and Engels offered socialist state officials and planners of the twentieth century a negative model of modern industrial urbanism: a guide of how and what *not* to build. That negative model carried into the twentieth century as architects, urban planners, and state officials continued to define the socialist city against Western, capitalist examples, especially the

United States. On the other hand, socialist urban experts nonetheless drew inspiration, ideas, and practices from capitalist cities. The socialist city was not a closed site, sealed off from the world beyond socialist borders. Rather, these cities existed in conversation and competition with global urban developments, from anticolonialism to capitalist consumerism.

Socialism was one of the great globalizing forces of the late twentieth century and socialist urbanism was among the many vectors through which socialist globalism spread. Recent scholarship approaches global socialist networks of this era as a form of "alternative globalization," running alongside and rivaling Western capitalism. In reclaiming the term "globalization," historians James Mark, Artemy Kalinovsky, and Steffi Marung write that "the idea of Western capitalism as the only engine of globalization bequeathed a distorted view of socialist and postcolonial states as inward-looking, isolated, and cut off from global trends until the capitalist takeover in the 1980s and 1990s. Such accounts ignore not only the agency of so-called peripheries in the creation of global interconnection but also the possibility that interconnection between peripheries might be considered a form of globalization similar to the intensification of interaction between 'the West and the rest'" (2020, 2). Thinking globally about socialist cities allows us to recover these global interconnections.

1.3 Overview

This Element explores the history of urban planning, city building, and city life in the socialist world. It synthesizes the wealth of scholarship on socialist cities that has been produced across disciplines over decades. I have been able to recount in this Element the experiences and textures of socialist urbanism thanks to the work of a multidisciplinary and multigenerational community of scholars. Their books and articles illuminate collectively the history of efforts in the previous century to make cities socialist.

This Element explores the urban history of the socialist world during the twentieth century. The Element opens with a section on the early socialist cities of the Soviet Union. This section highlights cities from Moscow to Magnitogorsk to Zaporizhzhia to introduce readers to the key features of Soviet urban development in the 1920s and 1930s. In subsequent sections, the Element explores socialist city development and urban life in the years after 1945 in the USSR and in newly socialist regions beyond. Drawing on recent scholarship by historians of socialism in Eastern Europe, Africa, Asia, the Middle East, and Latin America, later sections take a comparative approach while also highlighting examples of transnational exchange and competition. Finally, the Element concludes with a section on the continued significance of socialist urbanism today.

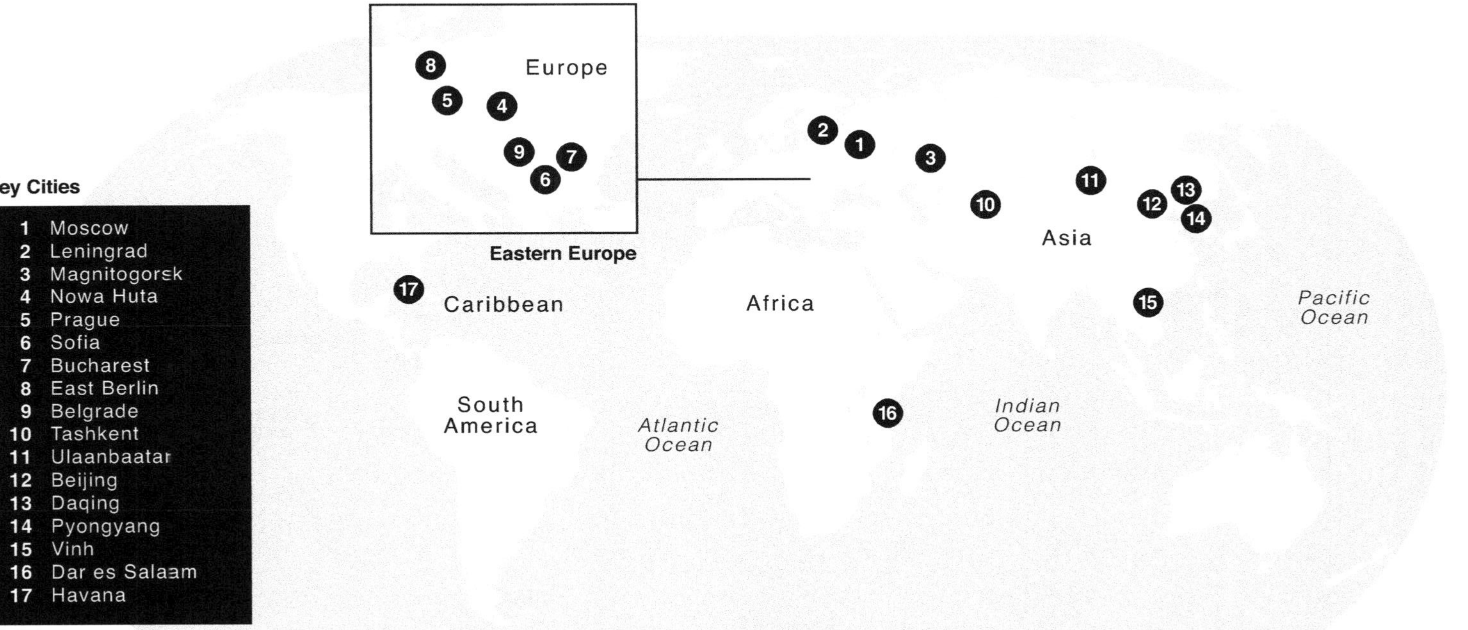

Map 1: World Map showing key cities discussed in the Element. Cartography by Gregory T. Woolston.

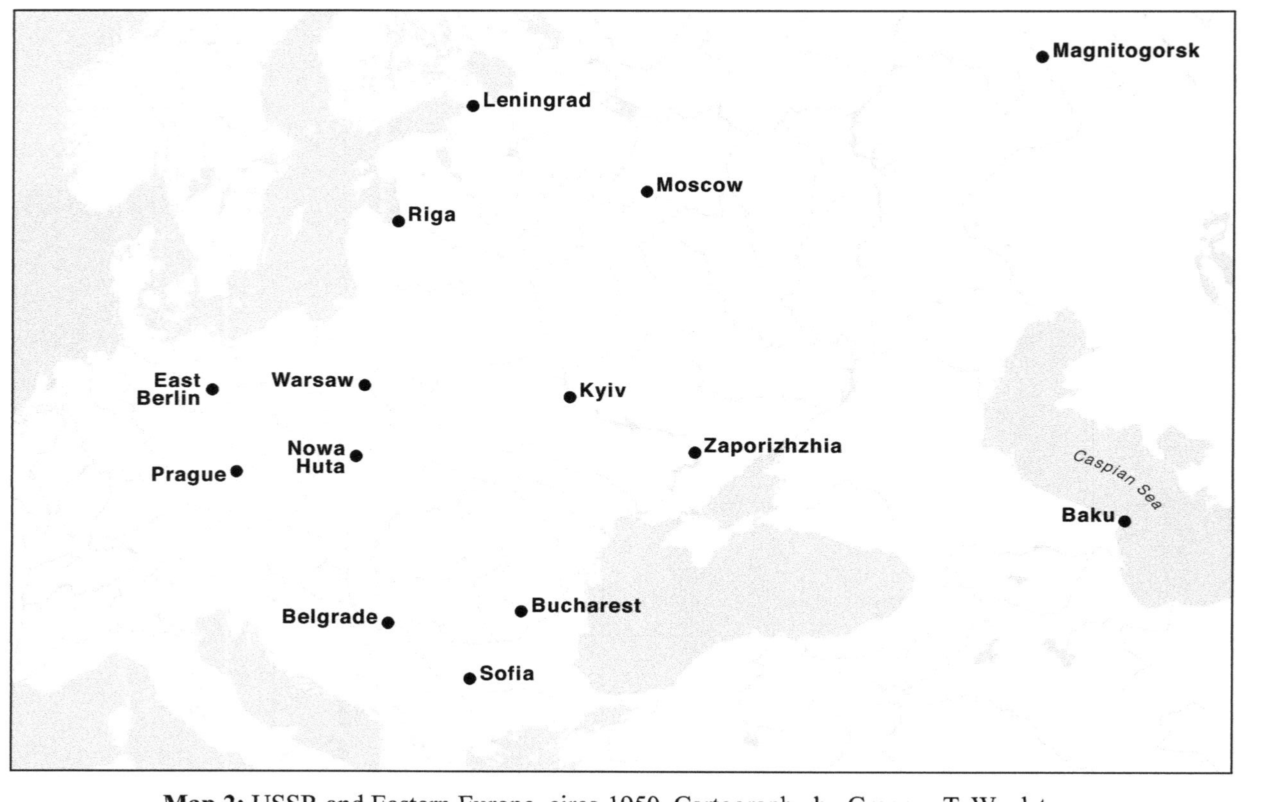

Map 2: USSR and Eastern Europe, circa 1950. Cartography by Gregory T. Woolston.

In addition to offering a historical overview of socialist urban development, this Element advances several arguments. First, the Element argues that socialist cities were "global" by design. Conceived as tools of world revolution, socialist city plans were intended as documents that could travel, adapt, and take root in a wide variety of geographies and cultural contexts. The global success – and lack of success – of the socialist approach to urbanism will be discussed throughout the Element. Second, this Element argues that one of the defining characteristics of the socialist city can be found in the new relationships that were forged in these spaces between planners and urbanites and between citizens and the state. While the Element examines high-level discussions among state officials and planners, it also asks what daily life was like in socialist cities. The rapid urbanization rates characteristic of the socialist world meant that in the early years many socialist city dwellers were new arrivals from rural or semirural spaces. The role that cities played in transforming urbanites into socialist citizens was central to the larger revolutionary project. Cities were also crucial sites of surveillance and control in socialist states. This Element scrutinizes not just ideal urban plans, but also daily realities and experiences on the ground.

Third, this Element highlights the important points of connection, competition, and urbanist exchange that persisted through the twentieth century between the socialist and capitalist worlds. Making socialist cities distinctive – by solving the perceived problems of capitalist cities – was always a priority for socialist planners and officials. Yet, relationships with the capitalist world persisted. Even at moments of Cold War tension, socialist architects routinely looked beyond the socialist sphere for inspiration, interlocutors, and models. This Element proposes that by locating the socialist city within a Global Urban History we avoid exoticizing and ostracizing socialist urbanism – two tendencies that plague earlier histories of these spaces. Given the continued presence of socialist urban infrastructures and plans in cities around the world today, a global approach not only helps us to better understand connections in the past. It also aids us in understanding urban trends and issues common around the world in our present.

2 Showcase Soviet Urbanism

Walking across the sleek marble platform of Moscow's Mayakovsky metro station in 1939, the American visitors could not help but look up. Airplanes soared overhead in colorful ceiling mosaics set within brightly lit cupolas running the length of the station. Shimmering bands of steel, carefully rolled to conform to the platform's many arches, carried the station's aviation theme downward. The steel, sourced from a factory that made planes for the Soviet Red Army, added a modern feel to an otherwise traditional, marble-clad space (Friedman 2000). This was one of Moscow's first subway stations. It was named after the Russian futurist poet Vladimir Mayakovsky and it opened its doors to passengers in 1938, quickly becoming a space celebrated for ushering in a new socialist way of life. Construction of the Moscow metro began in 1931 and the first line opened to passengers in 1935. This was a vital piece of civil infrastructure, providing much-needed transportation to a city rapidly expanding with the daily influx of peasant newcomers streaming into the capital, escaping famine and dislocation from the Soviet countryside. Yet, the Soviet subway served an equally, if not more important social role. As historian Andrew Jenks writes, the metro was a tool "for teaching Soviet power and for converting peasants into docile urbanites" (2000, 698). Standing on the platform of Mayakovsky metro station, the American visitors had to admit that this was unlike any subway they had ever seen. Lucky for them, they did not have to travel far to see it; the station visited by hundreds of thousands of Americans in 1939 was a life-sized replica of the original, assembled in Flushing Meadows, Queens as part of the Soviet pavilion at the 1939 New York World's Fair.

Just a sixty-foot section of Moscow's Mayakovsky metro station was reproduced for the New York World's Fair, but the clever use of mirrors created the illusion that visitors were truly standing on an extended platform forty meters below the Soviet capital. The replica subway station was a favorite among the fair's visitors: the *New York Times* included it on its list of "most outstanding attractions" and *Time* magazine ranked the entire Soviet pavilion as the best in the fair's Foreign Zone (Swift 1998, 373). Inviting residents of New York City, the world's premiere capitalist metropolis, to feel and express awe and excitement at the sight of a socialist subway station was a bold move for the Soviet state a mere two decades into its existence. But by 1939, much had been achieved in socialist city building, not only in the Soviet capital of Moscow but in an expanding network of industrial cities dotting the vast territory of the USSR. And so, at the fair, along with exhibits highlighting record-setting Soviet feats in industry and aviation, Soviet curators displayed the transformation of their overwhelmingly rural country into a land of showcase socialist cities.

The Soviet pavilion at the New York World's Fair was neither the first nor the last time that the USSR flaunted socialist architecture and urbanism abroad. The world's first communist state invested heavily in promoting its new, revolutionary way of life to a global audience. Long before the onset of the Cold War, competition with "the West" was built into the development program of this country. In addition to the replica of the Moscow metro, the Soviet pavilion at the New York World's Fair featured an exhibit on the General Plan for the

Socialist Reconstruction of Moscow, initiated in 1935. Also on display were large-scale Soviet construction projects, like Dniprostroi, the hydroelectric dam begun in 1927 on the Dnipro River (Rassweiler, 1988). The Soviet pavilion also featured a diorama showing the construction of the country's new industrial city of Magnitogorsk, or Magnetic Mountain (Swift 1998, 369–370). A crucial part of Stalin's First Five-Year Plan of 1928–32, Magnitogorsk was built next to a massive iron and steel works, the construction of which was inspired by the world's largest iron and steel plant in Gary, Indiana (Kotkin 1997, 42; Crawford 2022, 121). Like the Moscow metro, Magnitogorsk served to propel the Soviet Union forward on its march toward communism, all while "catching up with and overtaking" the West, as the Soviet slogan of the 1930s put it.

Russian revolutionary leader Vladimir Lenin and his Bolshevik Party seized control of the former Russian empire in October 1917, plunging the region into civil war and ultimately creating their new USSR in 1922. Lenin's Bolshevik Party, renamed the Communist Party in 1918, rejected most aspects of Russia's Tsarist past, pledging to build a new political order based on Marxist ideology that would sweep aside "bourgeois" institutions and values, elevating the working class, or proletariat, to positions of power. Yet, as historian Michael David-Fox observes, the USSR's communist leaders inherited from their Tsarist forerunners "a perennial imperative to overcome backwardness vis-à-vis the Western powers against which they measured themselves" (2012, 9). The Bolsheviks took this imperative further than their predecessors, viewing the drive to catch up with the more "advanced" West through a Marxist lens. "The Bolshevik Revolution," David-Fox argues "aspired not to catch up but to overtake, to leap over the industrially advanced countries into a new, alternative modernity" (2012, 9). For the leaders of the new Soviet Union, making cities socialist was key to constructing this new world – a path they believed would lead, ultimately, to the "bright communist future." Soviet cities provided an infrastructure and framework for modern socialist life, as well as an active environment capable of shaping the behaviors and mores of new Soviet people. Cities were not neutral spaces; rather, they possessed the power to recast society in a revolutionary mold.

It is unlikely that American visitors to the New York World's Fair were cognizant of the revolutionary power attributed to everyday urban spaces in the Soviet Union. For most visitors, the use of a material like marble in a public transportation system was radical in and of itself. Most Soviet riders of the Moscow metro, similarly awed by these underground palaces, would have had a firmer grasp of the ideology that imbued infrastructure and the built environment in their country. By the 1930s, Socialist Realist narratives in film and literature depicted ordinary people in the process of transforming from "spontaneity" to "consciousness," or, from a state of unawareness of one's role in the revolutionary whole to a higher state of perception whereby the needs of the individual and the collective are one (Clark 2000/1981). These transformations often took place through migration from the countryside to the city. Tanya Morozova, hero of the Soviet film *The Radiant Path*, a musical comedy of 1940, models this metamorphosis well. An illiterate domestic servant working at a village inn, Tanya is inspired by a handsome engineer to quit her job working for a petty-bourgeois innkeeper and move to Moscow. Set in the early 1930s, *The Radiant Path* follows Tanya as she arrives in the Soviet capital, finds work in a textile factory, learns to read, prevents a coworker from sabotaging production, and gains mastery over the weaving machines at her factory, eventually receiving the Order of Lenin for her record-breaking work. Tanya also becomes a Stakhanovite, a member of the movement named after miner Aleksei Stakhanov, whose record-breaking work the Communist Party encouraged others to emulate. Tanya sings several catchy tunes along this journey and in a final magical scene, she is pictured driving in a flying car above Moscow. As yet unbuilt structures from Moscow's "socialist reconstruction," still underway when the film was released, are shown completed on the cityscape. This is the bright communist future, peopled by new Soviet men and women like Tanya.

The New Moscow that the fictional Tanya Morozova inhabited was an ideal place where ideology and infrastructure overlapped with "breathtaking audacity," as Caroline Humphrey puts it. "After the Revolution," Humphrey explains, "architecture became one of the key arenas of ideology. In the 1920s, it was actually believed that carefully designed living quarters, for example, could eliminate the conditions for individualistic and *meshchankie* (petty-minded bourgeois) ways of life, and on this basis, a new human type would become the norm: Socialist Man and Socialist Woman" (2005, 39). As Humphrey notes, this goal was difficult to achieve and the scholarship on Soviet urbanism and everyday city life has long highlighted the gulf between plan and reality, emphasizing the tactics and survival strategies that ordinary people used to bypass, avoid, and counter official Soviet ideology (Bater 1980; Kotkin 1997). Nonetheless, Humphrey encourages us not to cast aside the power of the socialist-built environment and its relationship to ideology too quickly. These spaces, we are reminded by Humphrey, Murawski (2018), Zarecor (2018), and others, continued to guide and delimit behaviors and practices even when the blueprint differed from reality. Moreover, the idea that socialist cities would help bring about a new way of life became powerful dogma, traveling from the Soviet Union outward in the second half of the twentieth century.

The Soviet Union collapsed in December 1991 after existing for nearly seven decades. Soviet leadership, policies, and daily life changed significantly over time. The country remained consistent, however, in its commitment to city building and urban life. While Soviet officials, architects, planners, and not least residents struggled with numerous problems in their cities, from lack of housing to challenges of spatial control and management, the USSR's vision for the communist future was urban. This was not the case in all socialist states that emerged in the twentieth century, as later sections will discuss. When viewed comparatively, the Soviet case stands out for its urbanness. Associating rural life with backwardness, Soviet leaders aimed to propel their country forward toward communism by building cities. They routed resources, from building materials to food, into urban centers, exacting punishing policies on the countryside from at least the period of Stalin's First Five-Year Plan of 1928–32, which aimed to rapidly industrialize the country while forcibly collectivizing agriculture. This section explores the history of Soviet cities, with a focus on the Stalinist 1930s. Surveying key features of Soviet urban development at this foundational moment, it begins in the historic city of Moscow before examining new industrial centers founded during the period of the First Five-Year Plan. Planning strategies differed between historic and new Soviet spaces, but in all cases, the Stalinist approach to socialist city building shaped urbanism in lasting ways that remain visible on the cityscapes of these metropolises even today.

2.1 The New Moscow

Founded in the twelfth century, Moscow was nearly 800 years old when Soviet planners began work on the city's "socialist reconstruction." The existing urban fabric of the city placed real constraints on planning. Still, the historic city of Moscow, once the seat of the Muscovite Tsars, was reimagined in the 1930s as the "New Moscow," one of the youngest Soviet spaces, reborn through its socialist refashioning. Like other Soviet cities, Moscow grew rapidly as Bolshevik leaders established power over the territory of the former Russian empire. In 1914, the city covered an area of just under 6,000 hectares and had a population of about 1.8 million. By 1939, Moscow had nearly tripled in size as the population of the city reached 4.5 million. Much of that growth dated to the Stalinist 1930s. Moscow grew more still, in population and territory, in the postwar period. By 1957, when residents of the city were beginning to feel the effects of the liberalizing "Thaw" that followed the death of Stalin, Moscow's territorial boundaries had reached an area twice as large as before the Second World War. The city continued to expand into nearby towns and rural spaces so that by 1991, the year of the USSR's dissolution, the metropolis encompassed over ninety thousand hectares. The year the Soviet Union fell apart, Moscow had a population of just over 9.5 million.

The continual influx of people and the swallowing up of surrounding towns and villages posed a recurrent set of problems for generations of Moscow's planners as they sought to balance the symbolic role of the capital against the more mundane needs of residents. Moscow's rapid urban growth was not unique. While in 1917 one-sixth of all Russians were urban dwellers, by the 1980s two-thirds of Soviet citizens lived in cities (Bater 1980). The Soviet Union, with its drive from the late 1920s to industrialize rapidly and its harsh treatment of agrarian and nomadic populations, was a power bent on urbanization. Amidst the new country's broader urban development, Moscow served as a showcase socialist city and a model to be emulated elsewhere in the Soviet Union and beyond. The Soviet capital was designed with a global audience in mind.

Soviet decrees and urban planning debates of the 1920s and 1930s set the course for planning in Moscow and other cities for the duration of the Soviet period. Planners grappled not just with how to transform urban space to suit new, socialist needs and priorities but also how to treat older, prerevolutionary features of the city. Moscow's centuries-long development lent it the distinctive radial structure and the thick stone walls of an early modern fortified town. The center of Russia until the era of Peter the Great, Moscow lost its status as the state capital in the early eighteenth century, with the founding of St. Petersburg (Leningrad from 1924 to 1991) to the north. But Moscow remained an important cultural, economic, and religious center in the expanding Russian empire. In the late eighteenth century, Empress Catherine II sought to transform Moscow into a modern European city, recasting it as a stage for her enlightened politics (Martin 2014). The nineteenth century would then usher in the construction of railroad stations and tram tracks, the replacement of wooden structures with newer brick buildings, and the growth of industrial enterprises in the city. At the turn of the twentieth century, Russia's wealthy merchants built art nouveau mansions along the curving lanes north of the Moscow River inside the city's Garden Ring – a road that continues to delimit the city center today.

As the Bolsheviks nationalized property after 1917, the state swiftly took over many of Moscow's aristocratic and merchant estates, its theaters, concert halls, and other cultural institutions, and the former bureaucratic offices located in the city center. The new Soviet state also confiscated the holdings of Moscow's many monasteries with their golden-domed cathedrals that dotted the cityscape, and it began to manage the workers' districts and factories located to the north of the Garden Ring and in the southern part of the city. The decision taken in 1918 to locate the headquarters of the new state within Moscow's walled Kremlin ensured that this sacred Russian space would remain the centerpiece of the new Soviet capital. Eventually, in 1935, ruby-colored stars would replace the gold eagles of the Romanov dynasty that had long perched atop the towers of the Kremlin's ramparts, further transforming the fortress into a bastion of Soviet, and Stalinist, power. And over time, a handful of modern buildings would be constructed within the Kremlin walls to host state proceedings and Communist Party congresses. But the decision to use this space, along with nearby Red Square, as the symbolic heart of Soviet power signaled this socialist state's interest in using history, selectively, as a tool. In the early 1950s, when the leaders of newly communist China were faced with a similar decision about where to locate their headquarters, Soviet advisors in Beijing recommended that they use the Forbidden City. In the postwar years, the Stalinist state's disposition toward the past would be exported to the growing socialist world along with financial support, building materials, and urban plans.

Moscow's old trading highways connecting the Kremlin to historic Russian cities many kilometres away were similarly incorporated as key features of the first systematic plan for the capital, the General Plan for the Reconstruction of Moscow, adopted in 1935. Some of these highways were renamed and widened into leafy boulevards, as in the case of Tver' Street, running northeast from the Kremlin. Originally named for the Russian city to which it led, Tverskaia became Gorky Street, renamed in honor of Maxim Gorky, the Soviet writer who played a key role in elaborating the tenets of "Socialist Realism" (Figure 2). To transform this central artery into a model Socialist Realist boulevard, builders widened Gorky Street to three times its original breadth, mimicking a technique used in Haussmann's remodeling of Paris one century earlier (Castillo 1994, 61). Moscow's older ring roads were also incorporated as key elements of the 1935 General Plan, and the concentric shape of the city was further developed in postwar plans that saw new rings added as traffic and population in the city increased. Moscow's Soviet-era planners rejected their city's Tsarist and "bourgeois" past on principle, yet this inheritance was incorporated liberally into Soviet city planning during the Stalin era, at times serving as direct inspiration for a new socialist urban aesthetic.

Moscow was the capital city of the USSR's Russian Republic, but it was also the capital of the vast and multinational USSR as a whole. In Moscow, Soviet multinationalism – and the Socialist Realist mantra "national in form, socialist in content" – was put on display at the All-Union Agricultural Exhibition (VSKhV, later known as the Exhibition of Achievements of the People's Economy or VDNKh), a large fairground opened in 1939. The Exhibition displayed the latest advances in Soviet agriculture to Muscovites and out-of-town visitors, while also showcasing the architecture of the country's

Figure 2 Gorky Street, Moscow, USSR. Album / Alamy Stock Photo.

diverse national groups in pavilions spread throughout the fairgrounds. Monumentalized versions of the vernacular architecture from the Soviet Republics and other national regions of the country were displayed at each national pavilion. In later years, new pavilions dedicated to Soviet industrial, technical, and extraterrestrial feats were added, but in the 1930s, the pavilions were dedicated to distinguishing the architectural traditions of the Armenian, Belarusian, Uzbek, Ukrainian, and other Soviet nationalities (Castillo 1997a). In this multinational theme park, Moscow flaunted its role as a powerful capital city that united diverse peoples through communist "anti-imperialism."

Experiments with socialist urbanism and elaborations of what it meant to live according to a new, revolutionary way of life were not just the concern of urban experts. Urban residents themselves experimented with collectivism in dormitories, communal apartments, hostels, and workers' barracks. As Andy Willimott shows in his study of urban communes created in the decade and a half after 1917, "communards" aimed to transform the home and revolutionize domestic work and gender relations, upending tradition to redefine daily life in new socialist terms. Determined to forge a "new way of life" (*novyi byt*), communards grappled with how best to overcome the inherited habits and conventions that still governed daily life. In addition to introducing new behaviors and ideas, a new way of life could be achieved through spatial transformations. Strategies included the reconfiguration of living space and "the creation of a 'red corner' (dedicated reading space) in an otherwise disheveled apartment" (Willimott 2017, 17). Efforts to achieve a radical break with the past also featured in planning debates of the 1920s. Not everyone agreed that cities were key to the communist future. The famous urbanist-disurbanist debate, which kicked off in 1929 in reaction to the First Five-Year Plan, saw theorists like Mikhail Okhitovich imagining a socialist future in which cities and centralization were done away with in favor of a new type of settlement – one that achieved maximum spatial dispersal across the territory of the USSR, with disurbanist dwellings conceived as "individual, single-story, light metal, moveable structures connected to national networks along a single road" (Crawford 2022, 135).

Stalin's ascent to power in the late 1920s saw Soviet officials assert ever greater control over urban planning and architecture, bringing an end to the more utopian experiments of earlier years. In April 1932, the Communist Party Central Committee decreed that all independent cultural organizations in the USSR were to be abolished, with unions established in their place for each branch of the arts. Two months later, the USSR Union of Soviet Architects was founded. Based in Moscow, the Union oversaw discussions and developments in the architectural profession across the country. Republic-level branches of the union were also created (at the level of the Russian, Ukrainian, and Armenian Soviet Socialist Republics, e.g.). At the municipal level, a Moscow union section was established to coordinate local affairs. In July 1933, the USSR Union of Architects began publishing its monthly journal, *Arkhitektura SSSR* (*Architecture of the USSR)*, which discussed Soviet developments and also contained some coverage of international architectural affairs. Alongside the institutional changes of the early 1930s, the doctrine of Socialist Realism was mandated for all the arts. In striving for an architecture that was "national in form, socialist in content," architects of the Stalin era eschewed the modernist design that thrived in the USSR in the 1920s, elevating neoclassical approaches and vernacular, traditional forms instead.

By the Stalinist 1930s, the Soviet capital's urban planners included in their ranks architects, engineers, and bureaucrats, as well as the USSR's top leaders, many of whom were directly involved in city planning. As Heather DeHaan shows in her work on the Soviet city of Gorky, the site of a large Soviet automotive plant founded in 1932, the legitimacy of the Soviet planning profession under Stalin "was grounded in [planners'] adherence to Party-imposed practices" (2013). Yet, while they rooted their work firmly in Marxist and socialist ideology, Soviet urban experts also drew on ideas from outside the socialist sphere. British urban planner Ebenezer Howard's Garden City, for example, was widely influential in the Russian empire and continued to inspire after 1917. As Catherine Cooke observes, Howard's interest in reconciling town and country while maintaining the advantages of both and his call for advancement through planning a "new era of social life" resonated with Russian revolutionary culture. This feature of Howard's work, Cooke writes, "struck a far more familiar chord in Russia than it did in Europe. A belief in the possibility of achieving just that global transformation to a *novyi byt*, a whole new way of life, had been a pervading theme of Russian social and philosophical thought long before it became a central tenet of Soviet policy" (1978, 362). Among those Soviet planners most connected to the Garden City movement was Vladimir Semenov, who oversaw the General Plan for the Socialist Reconstruction of Moscow.

The 1935 General Plan for the Reconstruction of Moscow was never fully implemented. Nonetheless, the plan had a lasting influence on Moscow, on other Soviet cities, and on cities in the socialist world more broadly. The 1935 General Plan did not call for the total remodeling of Moscow. Rather, it aimed to update key city features, services, and amenities while adhering to and honoring Moscow's historic terrain. Existing waterways would be developed, and embankments built up. The Moscow River would be lined with granite embankments and new paved streets would run alongside, creating vast new urban ensembles. Former aristocratic estates would be transformed into vast new public green spaces. Water from the Moscow-Volga Canal, begun in 1932, would be knitted into the fabric of the city through new waterways carved into open parkland and underground tunnels. All services and amenities were to be provided by the plan for a projected population of five million residents. New residential districts were planned beyond the city center. In Moscow's southwestern district, one million square meters of new housing was planned. The Moscow metro, already under construction in 1931, was brought under the auspices of the General Plan. It would form the centerpiece of a more streamlined transportation network linking up the city. No additional industry was to be allowed in Moscow. The General Plan aimed to redistribute the city's population more rationally, lowering density in the center while increasing it on the periphery. At the heart of the city, a new state headquarters, the Palace of Soviets, would be constructed. This structure would have been the tallest building in the world, had it been built to completion as planned (Zubovich 2021).

The Moscow General Plan of 1935 was to be completed within ten years of its adoption. Yet, while construction proceeded on some of the most visible and central projects, like widening Moscow's famous Gorky Street, the plan was ultimately stymied by a range of factors and events, not least of which were the Great Terror and the war. By 1935, the Soviet Union was becoming a more closed and controlled space. Stalin's First Five-Year Plan (1928–32) prompted the so-called "Cultural Revolution," which saw a new generation of Soviet-trained professionals participate in a party-driven attack on "bourgeois specialists," many of whom had been trained before the revolution of 1917, had opposed the Bolsheviks' seizure of power, and could not claim the working-class origins now so important for professional advancement. On the heels of the First Five-Year Plan's rapid industrialization and collectivization drives, an internal passport system was introduced. Now, a *propiska*, or urban passport or registration, was required for city dwellers. Soviet nationalities policy shifted in the 1930s as well from an approach that sought to foster "nation-building" in the country's non-Russian regions to a policy encouraging the elevation of Russian national culture and the forging of more hierarchical relations between Soviet nationalities (which included, for example, Ukrainian, Uzbek, Armenian, Russian, Azeri, and other groups) based on the principle of the "Friendship of the Peoples." Increased restrictions on movement and the emergence of social and ethnic hierarchies echoed in Soviet urban development and city life.

In the mid-1930s, Soviet state and party officials initiated a period of political violence known as the purges or the Great Terror. The mass arrests and executions of this era reached their apex in 1937. The terror had a lasting effect on all aspects of life in the USSR and its impact on urban space and city life can be measured in several ways. Few Soviet institutions were untouched by the continuous purging of staff and by the torrid atmosphere of workers informing on bosses and neighbors informing on neighbors. In Moscow, among the many individuals arrested and executed during this period was Vasilii Mikhailov, head of the organization in charge of building Moscow's Palace of Soviets (Zubovich 2021). Mikhailov lived in Moscow's House on the Embankment, a large residential complex built in the late 1920s and early 1930s for top state and party officials located across the Moscow River from the Kremlin (Slezkine 2019). This address saw an especially high number of arrests, usually carried out in the middle of the night. Yet, a database created by Russia's Memorial Society of victims of political repression in Moscow, searchable by address, shows that few corners of the Soviet capital were spared the punishing effects of Stalin's and other top officials' attempts to purge the country of alleged spies, traitors, and saboteurs.[2]

Urban spaces in the USSR were designed with questions of residential control and surveillance in mind. From the 1930s Soviet urban planning and construction went hand in hand with measures intended to quell disorder,

[2] Russia's Memorial Society, a vital historical and human rights organization, was liquidated by the Supreme Court of Russia on February 28, 2022. The organization's databases documenting political repression remain available online as of July 2022. The database pertaining to Moscow is still available at: https://mos.memo.ru (accessed July 15, 2022).

prevent crime, and control population movement. As Johanna Conterio writes, "the party and state combined repressive measures with positive measures to raise urban standards of living through investments in urban infrastructure and food supply, reserved for registered urban residents" (2022, 480). Public spaces, such as urban parks and green spaces became in the Stalinist 1930s tools of policing and control. As Conterio notes, "these spaces, especially streets, squares, green spaces, and transportation networks, in practice became subject to systematic surveillance, patrolling by police, and spot document inspections" (2022, 497). For those lacking the proper residency paperwork, these city spaces could be dangerous sites where run-ins with authorities could lead to arrest and perhaps imprisonment. This fate would not necessarily find a person banished from urban space altogether; plenty of urban construction projects across the USSR were built by laborers of the Gulag, the vast system of Soviet labor camps. Major works, like the Moscow-Volga Canal, which supplied water and electricity to Moscow, relied on incarcerated workers for their completion (Ruder 2018). The Soviet state's reliance on incarcerated labor for construction only increased in the years after 1945, when the country began rebuilding after a devastating world war.

2.2 New Soviet Cities

Looking back in 1967 on the first fifty years of urban planning in the USSR, planners working at the Moscow-based institute of city planning observed that their profession's work could be divided into two categories: first, the development and reconstruction of historic cities and second, the construction of entirely new towns (Shkvarikov 1967, 18). While the Soviet Union celebrated the "socialist reconstruction" of older cities like Moscow and Leningrad, the creation of new socialist cities was a special achievement. In theory, new cities offered architects and planners the opportunity to work with a blank canvas – an exciting proposition for experts eager to bring ideal city plans into reality. In practice, however, new cities presented considerable challenges for both designers and residents. In the USSR's early industrial cities, for example, economic and industrial goals often took priority over the needs of new residents and the visions of architects and planners (Kotkin 1997; Crawford 2022). As a result, a sharp contrast between an ideal plan and lived reality can be observed in many of the USSR's new socialist cities. Between 1926 and 1966, approximately 900 new cities were founded in the Soviet Union (Shkvarikov 1967, 317). New city building would continue apace thereafter, culminating in the construction in Soviet Ukraine of what is often dubbed "the last planned Soviet city" of Slavutych, built from 1986 to 1989 to rehouse workers of the

Chornobyl (Chernobyl) Nuclear Plant following the catastrophic nuclear accident of April 1986 (Gubkina 2016).

The rapid pace of the construction of new Soviet cities was tied directly to the country's economic goals: most of the USSR's new cities were built to support industrialization and natural resource extraction. Some, like the arctic coal-mining town of Vorkuta and the port city of Magadan on the Sea of Okhotsk, were founded in the early 1930s as Gulag camps, transforming only gradually and in later decades into non-carceral urban spaces (Nordlander 1998; Barenberg 2014). Starting in the late 1940s, dozens of "closed cities" were also established to support the Soviet nuclear, scientific, and defense industries. Home to an estimated 1.5 million residents, closed cities were spaces of relative privilege, absent from maps and hidden from the public until the fall of the USSR in the 1990s (Emeliantseva 2011; Siddiqi 2022, 190). While this next section will focus on examples of new Soviet cities developed in the 1930s, this longer history of Soviet new town construction is worth bearing in mind, since the phenomenon of settling new Soviet urban spaces continued well into the 1980s.

Magnitogorsk, or Magnetic Mountain, founded in 1929 on the banks of the Ural River, is among the best-known examples of new Soviet cities. Magnitogorsk was one of dozens of industrial cities established in mineral-rich regions of the USSR during the period of the country's First Five-Year Plan of 1928–1932. This era was characterized by enthusiastic, militaristic slogans pledging to mobilize workers to "overfulfill the plan." The era was also beset by a lack of construction materials and labor, tight budgets, and the rapid tempo of development, all of which constrained planners and architects in their quest to build new and revolutionary socialist cities. German city planner Ernst May, whose public housing project at New Frankfurt prompted Soviet officials in 1929 to invite him to the USSR, found his plans for Magnitogorsk stymied by realities on the ground. Instead of a rational and ordered socialist city (*sotsgorod*), Magnitogorsk emerged as a ramshackle space of barracks, tents, and mud, with little evident planning (Kotkin 1995).

Magnitogorsk was home by the early 1930s to a rapidly growing workforce employed at the city's towering new steelworks. Unlike the gleaming socialist steel town celebrated widely in Soviet newspapers, the early city was defined by its social segregation, as foreign specialists and party and industrial managers were housed in better facilities than the steel workers they supervised. While Stalinist social hierarchies took spatial form in Magnitogorsk, many Soviet workers, originally from the countryside, relied on rural skills to survive the early city's harsh conditions, thereby reversing the Soviet value system that prized urban over rural life. As Stephen Kotkin writes, Magnitogorsk's

Figure 3 Metallurgov Prospekt, Magnitogorsk, USSR. SPUTNIK / Alamy Stock Photo.

peasant-urbanites “helped prevent the rest of the town from starving and showed remarkable abilities to cope in what proved to be a difficult, even dangerous environment” (1995, 108). Eventually, a planned city took shape in Magnitogorsk (Figure 3), which remains a major Russian steel town today. Yet, with the construction of heavy industry at this site taking priority during the city’s foundational years, progress in residential construction was repeatedly sidelined and delayed (Crawford 2022, 216).

Magnitogorsk, located in the USSR’s Russian republic, has long been the classic example of Soviet urban development of the First Five-Year Plan era. Yet, this city was just one of many Soviet new towns built during this period of rapid industrialization. New socialist cities were constructed during this era across the country, with a high number founded in Soviet Ukraine. Given Ukraine’s economic centrality and abundant natural resources, this region, and eastern Ukraine in particular, saw both the development of existing cities, like Kharkiv, and the creation of new industrial and energy centers, like Zaporizhzhia.

Kharkiv, the capital of the USSR’s Ukrainian republic from 1922 to 1934, in fact, experienced both the development of its existing city center and the construction of a new industrial city bearing its namesake nearby. In Kharkiv’s historic center, numerous constructivist and modernist structures were built in the 1920s and early 1930s, making this city a key site in the history of avant-garde architecture. Among this modernist heritage is Kharkiv's State Industry office complex (Derzhprom), a constructivist structure celebrated as the first Soviet skyscraper upon its completion in 1928. During the First Five-Year Plan, Kharkiv was also chosen as the location for an enormous new tractor factory. Built ten kilometers outside Kharkiv's urban center, the Kharkiv Tractor Factory was staffed by workers living in "New Kharkiv," a socialist city built adjacent to the industrial site. Constructed between 1930 and 1931, New Kharkiv featured one of the USSR's first *zhilkombinat*, or housing block – a replicable design unit that would find full expression in standardized micro-districts built in cities across the Soviet Union by the 1950s. Designed as a linear city, with horizontally arranged industrial facilities separated from residential areas by a transportation corridor and a green band running through the center, New Kharkiv's first housing block featured two six-story dorms and six four-story buildings with multiroom units for families. Canteens, schools, and workers clubs also featured as part of the block, forming the basis of sociocultural infrastructure that aimed as much as the housing itself to forge a new way of life (*novyi byt*) among residents (Crawford 2022).

New Kharkiv represents a more successful socialist city (*sotsgorod*) than was achieved at Magnitogorsk. While in Magnitogorsk, plans famously fell short, at New Kharkiv planning ideas first articulated elsewhere, including at Magnitogorsk, were implemented more fully in practice. As Christina Crawford shows in her work on Baku, Magnitogorsk, and Kharkiv, early Soviet architecture and urban planning developed through experimentation and the transfer of ideas and practices, both from the West to the Soviet Union and from one building site to the next. As Crawford puts it, "socialist city theory was generated for Magnitogorsk and implemented in Kharkiv" (2022, 283). New Kharkiv's housing blocks brought plans unrealized elsewhere into reality. Both the socialist city and the tractor factory at New Kharkiv were built based on experiments in architectural standardization explored elsewhere first. This adaptive process, known as *priviazka*, would become a key feature of Soviet industrial and housing construction, finding its fullest expression in the late 1950s, with the adoption under Nikita Khrushchev of the USSR's mass housing campaign (Crawford 2022, 250).

Like New Kharkiv, the new industrial metropolis of Zaporizhzhia was built, starting in 1928, to support one of the large-scale sites of the First Five-Year Plan. Located on the banks of the Dnipro River, this city housed the builders and workers of Dniprostroi, the Dnipro Hydroelectric Station (DniproHES), built by Soviet and American engineers between 1927 and 1932. One of the showcase projects of the USSR's First Five-Year Plan of 1928–1932, DniproHES answered Vladimir Lenin's earlier call to electrify the Soviet Union. As Lenin famously put it in 1920, "communism is Soviet power plus electrification of the whole country." The dam would power Soviet industrial and agricultural development in Soviet Ukraine (Rassweiler 1988). In 1933, a large steel mill, Zaporizhstal, was also founded in the new city. In 1934, a new paved road connected Zaporizhzhia to the important industrial city of Dnipropetrovsk to the north (Portnov 2022, 206).

Zaporizhzhia was not built on empty land, but rather on the location of an earlier settlement. The former town of Oleksandrivsk, founded in 1770, was transformed during the period of the First Five-Year Plan into a socialist city. Zaporizhzhia's population more than quintupled between 1926 and 1939, when the city's population reached 275,000 residents. This incredible growth occurred at a time when the larger population of Soviet Ukraine decreased. Forced collectivization and the resulting Holodomor, or famine, catapulted the surrounding countryside into turmoil. As van Zon, Batako, and Kreslavaska write, Soviet officials prevented those fleeing desperate conditions in the countryside from finding haven in the region's new industrial cities. "The world of heroic efforts to build modern Zaporizhzhya and the world of repression and famine," they write, "seemed to be two completely different worlds" (1998, 10). Many of Zaporizhzhia's residents came from well beyond the surrounding region – as one of the key cities of Stalin's First Five-Year Plan, the population drew from across the USSR.

In 1941, the Dnipro Hydroelectric Station was destroyed. Soviet Red Army troops blew up the dam as they retreated, faced with the swift advance of the Wehrmacht into Ukrainian territory following the launch of Operation Barbarossa (Rassweiler 1988, 189). It was only in 1969 that work began on the reconstruction of the power station and in 1980 that DniproHES-2 was completed. While this facility was being rebuilt, the Zaporizhzhia thermal power station, still the largest plant in Europe, was constructed south of the city. In 1970, the smaller city of Enerhodar was founded to serve the thermal power plant and its workers. Since February 2022, these cities of eastern Ukraine – Kharkiv, Dnipro, Zaporizhzhia, and Enerhodar – have sustained significant damage from Russian missiles and, in the case of Enerhodar, from Russian occupation. These cities, like other places in this now war-torn region, will undergo a new era of postwar reconstruction – the planning and discussion for which is already well underway (Dyak 2023).

Back in 1945, Soviet architects and urban planners facing their own postwar era began to think about their work in increasingly global terms. The socialist cities built in the preceding decades in the Soviet Union, they argued, would serve as models for cities now under construction in the expanding socialist world. Moscow-based architect Karo Alabian articulated this sentiment in a speech he delivered in 1949 to a group of Soviet officials and planners gathered to discuss the future vision for the city of Moscow. Reflecting on what had been achieved in Moscow since the adoption in 1935 of this city's General Plan, Alabian noted that Soviet experience in socialist urban planning and construction was valuable not just for his own country, but for other countries as well. "I have in mind Bulgaria, Poland, Czechoslovakia, Romania and other republics," Alabian stated.[3] These new socialist countries could all learn a thing or two from Moscow, Alabian believed. It was fair to say, the Soviet architect contended, that Moscow was the first of its kind: a city without the "irreconcilable contradictions" of capitalism. As the Cold War intensified into the 1950s and as Soviet leaders worked to extend their country's "sphere of influence" over new territories, Soviet architects touted their achievements in city building as victories not just in the construction of socialism, but also against the capitalist West.

3 The Socialist City Goes Global

On June 2, 1953, the government of the Democratic People's Republic of North Korea (DPRK) organized a conference to discuss the reconstruction of the North Korean capital city of Pyongyang. Like other People's Republics established in Europe and Asia after 1945, the DPRK was socialist and, initially, Soviet-aligned. The country's close connection to the Soviet Union and to the growing list of states that now made up the socialist world was evident in the urban plan presented for Pyongyang. This city, once occupied by Japan and more recently leveled by US air strikes during the Korean War of 1950–53, would be rebuilt as a socialist metropolis. When they met to discuss Pyongyang's reconstruction in 1953, North Korean state officials and the country's Minister of Construction were joined by foreign guests, like the staff from the Embassy of the Polish People's Republic, who sent a report about the meeting back to Polish leaders in Warsaw. North Korea would rely on foreign assistance to rebuild after the war and the foreign guests who attended this meeting about Pyongyang's reconstruction were asked to make appeals to their governments about possible forms of assistance. For new socialist leaders, urban planning was an important tool for transforming society at home and for establishing connections with the wider socialist world abroad.

The plan for the reconstruction of Pyongyang in 1953 was to be completed over the course of eight years. Devised with Soviet assistance, the plan foresaw the creation of vast new parks, an industrial district to the south, and new symbolic spaces in the city center. According to this plan, created for

[3] Russian State Archive of Literature and Art fond 674, opis' 2, delo 342, list 3.

a population of 600,000, residents of Pyongyang would live in a denser, greener, and more ordered space than they had in the period before socialism. The city's inhabitants would relax in the parks of Moranbong Mountain, located on a hilltop in central Pyongyang. They would stroll the city center to visit Kim Il Sung Square, with its monument erected in honor of the leader who led the country from its establishment in 1948 and would continue in the position of supreme leader until his death in 1994. As envisioned in 1953, the new Pyongyang would feature a Stalin Avenue, with four to five-story buildings running the length of the broad and beautiful street. Stalin Avenue would culminate in Opera Square, with its new opera house and the monument to Stalin, who died in March 1953. A Mao Zedong Avenue would also be built, leading to Mao Zedong Square, with its monument to the Chinese communist leader. Aware of the extant hierarchies of their socialist world, the architects of Pyongyang's 1953 plan were careful to make Mao Zedong Avenue slightly less wide with slightly shorter buildings than Stalin Avenue located a few blocks away (Polish Report 1953). This urban planning document, presented to both a North Korean and foreign audience in 1953, served equally as a guide for Pyongyang's socialist reconstruction and as a schema representing North Korea's relationship with the expanding socialist world. In the coming years, as Gunsoo Shin and Inha Jung show in their work on housing construction in North Korea after 1953, other socialist states, including the USSR and the German Democratic Republic (GDR), would provide high levels of assistance to North Korea as this country sought to adapt a socialist way of life (2016).

As socialism spread to new regions of the world in the mid-twentieth century, most socialist states were united in the common experience of rebuilding after war. The Polish embassy staff present at the North Korean meeting of 1953 were personally familiar with the experience of war and with the challenges and opportunities of postwar reconstruction. Poland's communist leaders, in power from 1947 to 1989, had faced similar questions now facing North Koreans as they rebuilt the country after the Second World War. The Soviet Union, Poland, and other Eastern European countries had begun this process slightly earlier, and they could therefore serve as guides in this endeavor. As Polish embassy staff noted in their report, the plans for Pyongyang were being prepared "on the basis of the experiences of the Soviet Union and countries of people's democracy, with a particular focus on the construction of Stalingrad and Warsaw" (Polish Report 1953). Like Pyongyang, Stalingrad and Warsaw had seen vast swaths of urban terrain leveled during war, leaving enormous challenges as officials and planners worked to restore basic urban infrastructure while also rebuilding according to socialist principles.

The Second World War shifted the course of world history and precipitated the expansion of state socialism into new regions of the world. Having proven itself through victory against Nazi Germany, the Soviet Union emerged as a world superpower after 1945. The Red Army's continued occupation of territory in Eastern Europe after the war all but guaranteed the spread of communism into this region. In other parts of the world as well, including Asia, Africa, and Latin America, Communist leaders took power in the postwar period. As state socialism spread, so too did socialist urbanism. In the years after 1945, then, the Soviet Union was a formidable power, but it was no longer the world's only socialist state. What did this new power and plurality mean for the development of socialist cities? As this section explores, the USSR served starting at mid-century as a model for newly socialist countries. Yet, the spread of communism also brought alternative models to the fore. Chinese, African, and Yugoslavian communism presented alternative visions competing for dominance with Soviet ideas and assumptions about cities and city life. After 1945, rival visions for socialism and socialist cities emerged from different parts of the socialist world.

3.1 Socialist Cities in Central and Eastern Europe

Monuments commemorating the Soviet Red Army's victory against Nazi Germany in 1945 were among the first new urban elements erected in East European cities that signaled the arrival of socialism and the expanding Soviet sphere of influence. Such monuments, intended to mark cities as "socialist" spaces, began to appear in Berlin, Prague, and Warsaw in 1945, and in Budapest in 1946. More monuments to the Red Army were built in other cities in the region in the 1950s. Sofia's Monument to the Soviet Red Army, discussed in the 1940s, was built in 1954. In time, statues of Lenin and Stalin began to appear as well on the cityscapes from Berlin in the new GDR to Riga and Lviv, now located in an enlarged Soviet Union. Whether in city centers or on the grounds of new factory complexes constructed to pursue Soviet-style industrialization, statues and monuments helped proclaim new political allegiances and cement new ideological affinities between the Soviet Union and Hungary, Poland, the GDR, and each of the newly socialist countries in the region.

In the GDR, a main site in the socialist reconstruction of the eastern, socialist half of the divided city of Berlin was Stalinallee, a broad avenue like Moscow's Gorky Street that was lined with seven to ten-story buildings richly ornamented with classical detail (Figure 4). This leafy, tree-lined boulevard drew on Soviet planning principles, while also referencing German traditions. As Brian Ladd notes, the street, built starting in 1951, was constructed "in the tradition of Unter

Figure 4 Procession along Stalinallee in East Berlin in March 1953, the month that Soviet leader Joseph Stalin died. INTERFOTO / Alamy Stock Photo.

den Linden," pre-war Berlin's premiere historic thoroughfare (1997, 185). Drawing on local, national architectural and planning forms, in combination with Soviet Stalinist principles, was a key feature of this early socialist period in Eastern Europe and elsewhere. In 1961, East Berlin's Stalinallee was renamed Karl-Marx-Allee, signaling the transition toward de-Stalinization. The dictator's removal was not signaled too loudly, however. The monument to Stalin, erected on Stalinallee in 1951, was removed by cover of night, "leaving no sign by morning that anything had ever stood there" (Ladd 1997, 187). Similar trends in the Stalinization and de-Stalinization of urban space can be traced in the 1950s and 1960s across the newly socialist countries of the Eastern Bloc, as well as in the cities of Eastern Poland, the Baltic states of Latvia, Lithuania, and Estonia, and the formerly Romanian territories of Bessarabia and northern Bukovina, all of which were annexed and incorporated into Soviet territory during the war. The reconstruction of Kyiv, the capital of Soviet Ukraine, featured a broad Stalinist boulevard ensemble following the bombing in 1941 of the city's main thoroughfare, the Kreshchatyk. (Figure 5).

There were other ways that urbanites now living under communism registered political change as it resonated through the built environment. The shifting relationship between new communist states and the societies they sought to govern and transform could be felt in the dispossession, or nationalization, of land and property previously owned by businesses and individuals. New,

Figure 5 Kreshchatyk Street in Kyiv, Ukraine, no date. SPUTNIK / Alamy Stock Photo.

socialist ideas about public space, property, and communal life took hold across Central and Eastern Europe. Similarly, as former federal and municipal governments were ousted, their successors faced questions of where to locate the offices of the new state and Communist Party. Early on, existing buildings were used rather than new, purpose-built government structures – these, with the exception of Prague, would generally be built in the later, modernist period. Prague was unique in this regard. No large, new government headquarters were built in Prague and the city's historic center not only escaped major damage during the war, but also changed little during four decades of communist rule (Zarecor 2011).

For architects redesigning and rebuilding the newly socialist cities of Central and Eastern Europe, the most keenly felt change of the late 1940s and 1950s was the shift toward Socialist Realism. This doctrine, elaborated first in the Soviet Union in the 1930s, was imported into the architectural practice of Eastern Europe through didactic materials sent from Moscow, through study trips to Soviet cities, and through vague slogans about the need to build cities that were "national in form, socialist in content." Socialist Realist doctrine severely limited architectural and urban practice, preventing urban experts from engaging with modernist design traditions and approaches. At the same time,

Socialist Realism was adapted to each new place, rooting itself in local, vernacular design traditions. One solution to the problems raised by Socialist Realism was simply to cleave to the Soviet model directly, reproducing forms and buildings like those already built or under construction in Moscow. In the early 1950s, for example, buildings constructed on the model of Moscow's postwar Stalinist skyscrapers were built in Warsaw, Prague, Bucharest, Kyiv, and Riga.

Moscow's eight monumental skyscrapers, built on Stalin's orders starting in 1947, were the premiere architectural works underway in the Soviet capital after the war. Built during the first years of the Cold War, Moscow's towers were not called "skyscrapers" by Soviet officials and architects, but "tall buildings," a terminological choice that deliberately aimed to draw a line between socialism and capitalism (Zubovich 2021). From the perspective of Moscow's architectural theorists, the Stalin-era high-rise was the pinnacle of Socialist Realist design. With their neoclassical detail, monumental scale, and locations within cityscape "ensembles" of parkland and boulevards, these towers represented for Soviet architects the apex of Stalinist architectural achievement. The tallest of these buildings, Moscow State University, stood as a symbol of Soviet victory in the recent war and as a testament to Soviet supremacy on the world stage (Figure 6). Completed just months after Stalin's death in 1953, this imposing,

Figure 6 Lomonosov Moscow State University and gardens, Soviet Union, 1966.

tiered structure was a favorite stop on tours of the capital given to foreign guests in the 1950s.

Lev Rudnev, the same architect who designed Moscow State University, was soon dispatched to Poland to build a sister structure in Warsaw. This Polish skyscraper, the Palace of Culture and Science, officially opened to the public in 1955 (Crowley 2003, 37; Murawski 2019). Built by both Soviet and Polish workers, Warsaw's forty-two-story Stalinist skyscraper continues to dominate the cityscape of the Polish capital today. While the university building in Moscow serves an educational role, Warsaw's tower is more multifunctional, serving to bring the residents of the Polish capital together in a variety of activities. As Michal Murawski writes, "between 1955 and the end of 1990, 147 million people have taken part in 221,000 events within the Palace" (2019). Events, celebrations, parties, and protests continue at the site today.

In addition to Moscow's Stalinist skyscrapers, the Soviet capital city's General Plan of 1935 provided a blueprint for cities in Eastern Europe. The General Plan, in particular the plan's widened boulevards and its use of the existing cityscape to suit new socialist needs, served as a key point of reference for Romanian architects as they worked to craft a new master plan for Bucharest in the early 1950s (Grama 2019, 39–51). Soviet industrial new town construction similarly guided newly socialist states in Eastern Europe. The new city of Nowa Huta, Poland's "first socialist city," was built starting in 1949 outside Kraków. Constructed to serve the Lenin Steelworks, Nowa Huta was, like Magnitogorsk, home to a diverse population that included enthusiastic young workers eager to respond to calls to "build socialism" (Lebow 2013). The Soviet model of urban development and industry proved to be a powerful blueprint supporting the spread of socialism. Yet, as Katherine Lebow notes, Nowa Huta's "planners and professionals were able to carve out space for pursuing their own goals" (2013, 182). The transfer of ideas and expertise from the Soviet Union to new parts of the world was neither total nor unidirectional.

3.2 From the "Friendship Decade" in Sino–Soviet Relations to the Maoist Urban Model

In 1957, Soviet architect Dmitrii Chechulin traveled to China. Chechulin, the chief architect of Moscow from 1945 to 1949, toured the Chinese capital city, visiting its many historic landmarks. He had his picture taken at the Forbidden City, once home to emperors of China's Ming and Qing dynasties. This was not the first time that this Soviet architect engaged with China and with his Chinese colleagues. Just a few years earlier, Chechulin was one of numerous Soviet architects busy designing buildings for Beijing. Chechulin's International

House of Radio was constructed in the Chinese capital city in 1955 (Lokotko 2018, 42). A few years later, back in Moscow, Chechulin opened his Hotel Pekin (or Hotel Beijing). This structure, located above Moscow's Mayakovsky metro station, celebrated the Sino–Soviet friendship while also repeating in smaller scale the tiered shape of Stalin's postwar high-rises – structures that Chechulin himself had participated in building. Chechulin was one of thousands of Soviet experts and advisors who aided Chinese colleagues in the 1950s in their drive to build a socialist state. The architect was thus a participant in the "friendship decade" that characterized Sino–Soviet relations from the founding of the People's Republic of China in 1949 to the Sino–Soviet split that took hold by the early 1960s. By the time that Chechulin visited Beijing in 1957 the Sino–Soviet friendship was beginning to fray. Still, nearly a decade of Soviet influence in China had left a legacy in the built environment of this communist country, most notably in the capital city of Beijing.

Soviet experts who visited China during the "friendship decade" included engineers helping to rebuild China's rail routes in Manchuria, geologists aiding in the search for uranium deposits, and historians teaching military history to cadres of the People's Liberation Army (Kaple 2015, 49, 52, 67). Soviet experts also advised their Chinese counterparts on agricultural questions. Yet, as Yan Li writes, Soviet influence was "more visible in cities than in the countryside" (2014, 49). In her Element, *The Modern City in Asia*, Kristin Stapleton notes that Chinese Communists lacked experience in governing urban spaces, having "spent decades building their regime in rural base areas before they captured major Chinese cities in the years after WWII" (2022, 57). Importing urban expertise from abroad made sense, at least initially, though Chinese Communists did not share with their Soviet counterparts a common view of the positive revolutionary advantages of urban life. As Weiping Wu and Piper Gaubatz write, in China, where the communist revolution "relied upon a rural base [. . .] cities were portrayed as centers of consumption, which had fueled the rising inequality between rich and poor regions and people in China" (2020, 86).

Chinese Communists' rural orientation and "stigmatized vision of urban life" would continue to shape urban policies in the coming decades (Wu and Gaubatz 2020, 86). During China's Cultural Revolution of 1966–1976, and during the longer rustication movement, Chinese youth were dispatched to the countryside to "receive re-education from the peasants" and to relieve pressure on the country's rapidly growing cities (Pan 2002, 363). When the Chinese Communist Party (CCP) took power in 1949, less than 10 percent of the country's population was urban (Hou 2018, 203). Over the ensuing decades, Chinese leaders would struggle to control and at times restrain urban growth. They introduced measures like those adopted decades earlier in the Soviet

Union. The *danwei* (work unit) system that emerged in the 1950s saw the emergence of walled housing complexes containing housing and amenities for workers from a single factory or industry (Bray 2005). The *hukou*, or household registration system, codified in the legislation of 1958, curbed freedom of movement in China and tied citizens to either urban or rural residency through the introduction of residency permits. China's rural population is, as a result, prevented from freely settling in cities. As Kam Wing Chan and Will Buckingham write, the *hukou* system, still in place today, "is a cornerstone of China's infamous rural–urban 'apartheid,' creating a system of 'cities with invisible walls" (2008, 583). In China's "socialist market economy" today, the two-tiered *hukou* system remains in place as a lasting consequence of earlier communist reforms.

Despite real differences in how Soviet and Chinese communists viewed cities, in the decade after 1945, the Soviet Union attempted to exert considerable influence over the course of architecture and urban development in China and indeed throughout the expanding socialist world. The strength of this influence would diminish over time, but initially, the Soviet model held considerable sway. It could be seen in Beijing in February 1949, when a large banner was unfurled on Tiananmen Square in preparation for a rally held to celebrate the victory of the CCP, which had recently taken power in the city. The banner read: "In waves of red flags and jubilant songs, / A sea of people celebrates their liberation; / Common folks are now masters, / The Imperial Palace is transformed into a new Red Square" (Hung 2011, 25). Referring of course to Red Square in Moscow, China's new communist leaders signaled in their banner the close relationship being forged between China and the Soviet Union. They also signaled that they would repurpose, adapt, and reinterpret ceremonial urban spaces belonging to their predecessors in ways that would serve present needs and interests, as had been done a few decades earlier by Soviet leaders in Moscow. Later in 1949, when Chinese communist leader Mao Zedong formally announced the founding of the People's Republic of China, he did so atop the Gate of Heavenly Peace, on one side of Beijing's Tiananmen Square, built in the seventeenth century.

One of the concerns arising in newly communist Beijing – a concern that received special attention from Soviet architects – was the question of where to locate the headquarters of the Chinese communist state. While one group of Chinese architects advocated for the preservation of historic Beijing through the construction of a new administrative area outside the traditional city center (Hung 2011, 27), another group with Soviet support advocated instead that the new Chinese state make use of Beijing's historic center. Renovating an existing space would not only be less costly, they argued, but it also "would prevent the old town from deteriorating" (Hung 2011, 30). In the end, Chinese officials opted for the latter plan. They would live in new buildings constructed within Beijing's Imperial Palace precincts, with their offices located not far away. Nearby Tiananmen Square, built in 1651, would be renovated and expanded and by 1958, the square could hold up to 500,000 people. Just as the Lenin Mausoleum has stood on Red Square since 1924, the mausoleum of Mao Zedong has been on Tiananmen Square since 1976. As in socialist cities around the globe, renovated and newly venerated public spaces like these helped to mark cities as distinctly socialist.

In the areas of architecture and urban planning, Soviet experts advised their Chinese colleagues both by visiting China and by hosting them in the USSR. For Soviet experts, there was more to this period of exchange than simply sharing expertise with the goal of strengthening global communism. Soviet experts not only tended to earn higher wages in China than if they had stayed at home, but they also enjoyed the opportunity to leave the postwar USSR. Living in hotel accommodations far superior to their communal apartments back home, in going to China Soviet advisors escaped the harsh realities of rations and shortages that characterized life in a country still recovering from the recent war (Kaple 2015, 55). Like German and American experts who participated in the construction of the Soviet city of Magnitogorsk in the late 1920s and early 1930s, Soviet experts in China in the 1950s would experience amenities and luxuries that were out of reach for ordinary Chinese citizens.

For the CCP, the Sino–Soviet alliance served to mobilize Chinese society in the construction of Soviet-style socialism in China. The friendship between the two countries was celebrated in newspapers, pamphlets, and images circulated throughout the country hailing the Soviet Union as "the leading country in every regard," a country that had not just caught up with but surpassed the capitalist West, "a strong, advanced socialist country marching on the path to Communism" (Li 2014, 50). As Yan Li notes, the Sino–Soviet friendship was also displayed in more concrete ways through transformations to urban space. Between 1958 and 1960, Ten Great Buildings were constructed to celebrate the tenth anniversary of the People's Republic. Among them was the Military Museum of the Chinese People's Revolution, the shape and spire of which clearly referenced Moscow's Stalinist architecture (Figure 7).

Soviet influence was also prominently displayed in buildings like the Soviet Union Exhibition Center, designed by Soviet architect Sergei Andreev and completed in 1954 just outside the northwestern gate of Beijing's city wall. "The impact of the complex," Peter Rowe and Seng Kuan note, "was unmistakably monumental, visually underscoring the new Soviet presence in China" (2004, 92). Art historian Wu Hung recalls the excitement that this building, with

Figure 7 Military Museum building in Beijing, China, no date. Christian J Kober / Alamy Stock Photo.

its tall gold spire, inspired in him and others, who "competed to put their names on the waiting list" to see the "enormous exhibition, showing off the Soviet Union's wondrous achievements in all aspects of its economic, cultural and social life" (2005, 105). The exhibition center was quintessentially Stalinist, with its tall central tower and neoclassical colonnades. Yet the exhibition center was completed at the dawn of a new era; the building opened in time for the first visit to China by Nikita Khrushchev, Stalin's successor. Khrushchev would oversee the most active years of the "friendship decade," before his de-Stalinization campaign begun in 1956 soured relations between the USSR and China.

The Soviet Union was not the sole influence guiding urban development in early communist China. Chinese architects and planners also drew on their past experiences designing and building in the decades following the collapse of the Qing dynasty in 1911, when China was very open to foreign influences and many Chinese studied abroad (LaCouture 2021). Additionally, the new communist state made use of infrastructure and city spaces built up during Japanese colonial rule. In his study of Anshan, an industrial city in China's northeast (Manchuria), Koji Hirata shows how the Anshan Iron and Steel Works, founded by Japan in the 1910s, made Anshan one of the most important industrial centers of Maoist China. As Hirata writes, "the CCP construction of industrial cities built upon legacies from the pre-1949 regimes" (2023, 102). Chinese communist officials inherited in Anshan not only the steelworks, but also Japanese-built housing. Upscale homes in the residential district of Taiding soon housed CCP cadres, creating a sharp divide between the living standards enjoyed by party officials and those endured by workers. As in Soviet industrial cities, like Magnitogorsk, Chinese leaders prioritized industrial needs over the construction of new housing badly needed for Anshan's rapidly growing population of industrial workers. Socialist cities in early communist China were thus sites of social segregation – a reality as difficult to square with socialist values as it was common across the socialist world.

A turning point in socialist city building in China was marked in the 1960s by the construction of the new city of Daqing. Located near Harbin in the country's northeast, Daqing was built for workers in the oil industry. The city quickly became a symbol of Chinese industrial modernity and self-reliance, with the new slogan circulating widely in China encouraging citizens to "learn from Daqing" (Figure 8). The city's "new socialist men and women" served as models for those in the rest of the country. As Hou Li writes, "there is no other place in China where the physical landscape and the people's everyday lives were more intertwined with state interests and ideological debates. It is the

Figure 8 "Study the Daqing spirit and steadfastly maintain the guiding principle of autonomous initiative and self-reliance," Chinese poster, English translation by Kristin Stapleton. Album / Alamy Stock Photo.

place where the communist utopia and the people's revolutionary spirit sought to conquer reality" (2018, 2). Daqing contributed over half of China's annual crude oil production, making the city vital to strengthening the country's economy and global stature. The mobilization of workers in Daqing is reminiscent of similar industrial endeavors pursued earlier in the Soviet Union and other socialist states. To prepare the oil field for production, "armies" of workers were sent to join the "battle" in one of five "sub-battlefields." Youth volunteers and workers' family members busily constructed housing using a dry-pounded earth technique learned from local peasants. Known as *gandalei*, this housing was cheap and quick to build and could be usefully located alongside worksites (Hou 2018, 51–56).

Daqing can be compared to the Soviet oil town of Baku, the city on the Caspian Sea that was vital to the USSR's economy and was one of the first Soviet urban spaces to undergo a formal general planning process (Crawford 2022). Yet, as Hou Li notes, in its first few decades, Daqing did not have a master plan. Daqing consisted of various settlements spread out at points along the oil field, a belt-shaped 140-kilometer expanse that continually shifted as drilling moved into new areas. It was only in 1980, when the city's non-agricultural population had reached almost half a million, that Daqing was granted city status and a first master plan was created. As Hou notes, the plans adopted for Daqing were always subject to the needs of the oil industry (2018, 200–201). In another decade and a half, the city's population would reach 1 million, but even with an urban plan in place, the city was subservient to industry, with residential districts abandoned as needed as the oil field encroached into urban terrain (Hou 2018, 200). Into the 2000s, Daqing continued to expand and develop in response to the diversification of the city's economy from oil and gas extraction toward petroleum processing and petrochemical industries (Li et al. 2015). Residential construction more recently evolved from the city's signature *gandalei* residences to prefabricated concrete dwellings (Figure 9).

In February 1965, the Chinese Premier Zhou Enlai and Soviet leader Aleksei Kosygin met to address issues including the ongoing conflict in Vietnam, Laos, and Cambodia. Sino–Soviet relations had been strained since at least 1960 and the two countries had much to discuss. On their way to Kosygin's hotel in Beijing, the two state officials had a few moments to talk. This was Kosygin's first visit to Beijing and he could not help interrupting the more serious topics of conversation to pose questions about what he was seeing outside the car window. Why did the workers' residences have a wall around them, Kosygin asked. What was this factory, what is this monument, and how is the lighting inside that building? And finally, "This is the Council of Ministers? . . . Comrade Zhou

Figure 9 Chinese oil workers apartments, Daqing oil town, Heilongjiang Province, China, 2016. Alain Le Garsmeur China Archive / Alamy Stock Photo.

Enlai, you have occupied the area of the imperial residence."[4] According to the interpreter's transcript of this conversation, Kosygin laughed. "Your Kremlin, too, belonged to the emperor in the past!" Zhou replied. Kosygin's comments to Zhou reflect the significant changes that had taken place in Soviet architecture and urbanism. They also reflected how little Kosygin knew about Soviet efforts to shape the global course of socialist city building in earlier years. By 1965, a new model for socialist urbanism had taken precedence, one based on prefabricated construction rather than classical historically influenced design.

3.3 Socialist Mass Housing as a Global Phenomenon

In December 1954, an important Soviet conference was held in Moscow on architecture and construction. The Builders' Conference brought together Soviet construction managers, engineers, architects, and planners, as well as representatives from these professions in other socialist countries, including the GDR, the DPRK, and the Mongolian, Polish, Czechoslovak, Romanian, Hungarian, and Bulgarian Peoples Republics.[5] Held one year after Stalin's death, this conference ushered in major changes in Soviet urban design – changes

[4] "Record of the First Contact between Premier Zhou and Vice Premier Chen Yi and Kosygin," February 6, 1965, History and Public Policy Program Digital Archive, PRC FMA 109–03957-04, 1–21. Translated by Stephen Mercado. http://digitalarchive.wilsoncenter.org/document/165488.

[5] Russian State Archive of the Economy fond 339, opis' 1, delo 1039, list 2.

that would profoundly affect the lives of Soviet urbanites while also influencing and responding to global trends in construction. In the final few days of the conference in 1954, those in attendance witnessed Soviet leader Nikita Khrushchev publicly dress down the big wigs of Stalinist architecture in an auditorium of their peers. Unhappy with the course of Soviet architecture and urban planning under his predecessor, Khrushchev railed against the waste of public funds and the "excesses" of Stalinist construction and design, calling instead for the abandonment of architectural flourishes and the introduction of cheap and more rapid industrialized methods of construction.

Khrushchev's influence on Soviet architecture and urban construction was significant, but it would not be accurate to give him full credit for the new approaches pursued in this field from the mid-1950s onward. As Mark B. Smith shows, Khrushchev's remarks at the Builders' Conference, published in the Soviet press following the conference, gave the green light to changes and experimentation already underway in the Soviet building industry (2010; also Bocharnikova 2014). Still, during his tenure, Khrushchev actively worked to shift Soviet priorities away from monumental projects like Moscow's Stalinist skyscrapers and toward less vertical, though still ambitious, endeavors like the campaign to build prefabricated housing on a mass scale. Initiated by state decree in 1957 with the goal of eradicating the USSR's housing crisis within ten years, Khrushchev's mass housing campaign moved Soviet families out of communal living spaces and into single-family apartments built rapidly and affordably using standardized designs and prefabricated elements and materials. In addition to transforming Soviet urban space, the mass housing campaign also diminished the role and status of individual architects. As Nikolai Erofeev observes, the architect Nikolai Rozanov, celebrated in 1974 in the Soviet architectural press for his role in "building more dwellings than anyone else in the USSR," remains a largely unknown figure (2019, 207). In 1958, Rozanov, responsible for the creation of a staggering 2.4 million dwellings, developed the prototype of the I-464, one of the most widely used Soviet serial housing delivery systems. The I-464 building system was not only used throughout the USSR. It was exported to a range of countries from Yugoslavia to Afghanistan to Cuba (Erofeev 2019; Erofeev and Stanek 2021).

Philipp Meuser and Dimitrij Zadorin write that Soviet mass housing from this era is "usually blamed for creating the most monotonous built environment in the history of mankind" (Meuser and Zadorin 2015, 7). Indeed, the repetition that prefabrication introduced to urban space was even a subject of Soviet comedy. A popular film of 1976, *Irony of Fate*, is based on the premise that a man from Moscow, having drunk too much with his friends on New Year's Eve, could accidentally board a flight to Leningrad, hop in a cab and wind up in someone else's apartment, which looked almost identical to his own back in the capital city. Khrushchev's lofty goal of solving the USSR's housing crisis was never fully achieved and his policy became the butt of jokes, but the USSR's mass housing campaign transformed daily life in the Soviet Union for tens of millions of people, often for the better. As Steven Harris notes, Khrushchev's mass housing campaign was part of the larger shift away from the upheavals and suffering of the Stalin era. "In the Khrushchev era," Harris writes, "people's lives became decidedly less turbulent and less violent, and more settled and more normal, which in itself was an extraordinary thing" (2013, 20). The move from a communal to a single-family apartment was a defining feature of Soviet life for many in the years after Stalin's death.

The effects of the Soviet mass housing campaign were immediately visible, as cranes rose on cityscapes across the USSR and hopeful urban residents joined waitlists for new single-family apartments. Between 1958 and 1964, the Soviet Union had the highest per capita rate of housing construction in Europe (Smith 2010). Most of the new construction would initially take the form of five-story blocks of apartments designed for single-family occupancy. Nicknamed 'khrushchevki' after the Soviet leader, these five-story residential blocks were located in new neighborhoods, or microdistricts, on the outskirts of existing cities. In Moscow, much of this new residential construction was carried out in the southwest and northern regions of the capital. Moscow's Novye Cheremushki district served as a model for this new direction in Soviet building. Located in the city's southwest, the district became famous across the USSR as many of the principles applied here were adapted and repeated elsewhere. The so-called Ninth Experimental District in Novye Cheremushki, built from 1956 to 1959, was among the most famous attempts to build according to the new approach. On a twelve-hectare block, the Ninth District was made up of fourteen mainly four-story residential buildings designed for a population of just over 3,000 residents. An additional three eight-story buildings were added to the district in the later stages of construction (Bocharnikova 2014). The Ninth District had grocery stores, a cafeteria, a telephone exchange, a nursery, a kindergarten, a school, and a cinema. It was landscaped with green spaces and small parks for the use of residents (Anderson 2015). Early designs like this led to the construction of even larger microdistricts for up to 12,000 residents. The goal of these new living spaces was not merely to make use of inexpensive materials and rapid construction methods. These places were also intended to promote communal values and the "communist way of life."

The Soviet Union's new mass-produced housing districts made the country's cities more alike, but differences also emerged as prefabricated building systems were applied in one place and then another. Paul Stronski notes that in the

USSR's Uzbek republic, Soviet planners confronted early on the need to adapt standardized designs to local Central Asian conditions (2010). Heat, sun, and seismic activity, like the 1966 earthquake that left 300,000 residents of the Uzbek capital of Tashkent homeless, were all factors to consider when building in this region. In Tashkent, Samarkand, and other Uzbek cities, Khrushchev-era planners grappled not only with climate and geography but also with how to adapt standardization, often designed with Soviet Russians in mind, in ways suiting the cultural needs of Uzbeks. How could planners reconcile the goals of the single-family socialist apartment with the extended-family homes that made up the Uzbek *mahalla*, the traditional Islamic neighborhood community? How could the daily customs and decorative preferences of Uzbeks be incorporated into the design of prefabricated housing districts? "In the Khrushchev era," Stronski explains, "one began to hear the argument that Uzbeks could be made into apartment dwellers, but only if planners made concessions to Central Asian cultural needs in planning buildings" (2010, 227). Design institutes in Tashkent, as in other regional centers, experimented with introducing new elements to prefabricated systems, from shading devices and balconies to decorative mosaics on façades. As it happened, these elements would be used also outside the USSR, in cities like Accra, as Soviet residential prefabrication traveled to other parts of the globe (Stanek 2020, 80).

The standardized apartment block fundamentally transformed life in the socialist world from the 1950s onward, but other forms of residential construction continued during this period as well. In Tashkent, the nine-story residential blocks of Chilanzar, the city's model mass housing district completed in 1959 without serious consideration of residents' needs, held little appeal, initially at least, for local residents (Stronski 2010, 220–223). There were alternatives to the mass housing construction carried out largely on the outskirts of cities like Tashkent. Private house construction continued during the Khrushchev era as well, both in Tashkent, in other Uzbek cities, and indeed across the USSR. In the Uzbek republic, Samarkand's traditional city center, for example, was expanded from the 1960s–1980s through the construction of new adobe brick residences featuring traditional Central Asian courtyards (van der Straeten and Petrova 2022, 298). The socialist city was characterized by both change and continuity. Prefabricated construction did not wholly supplant older and more traditional city spaces.

Prefabricated housing districts, widespread across the Soviet Union by the late 1960s, varied in their application by region. They also served a diverse array of state goals, from making residents more socialist to supporting natural resource extraction in underpopulated regions. The city of Cheremushki, located by the Sayano-Shushenskaya hydro power station in Siberia

(Figure 1), is one example of this link between standardized housing and resource mining. Nurek, a city built in the 1960s in the Soviet Republic of Tajikistan, provides yet another example. In his study of Nurek, Artemy Kalinovsky shows that Khrushchev-era mass housing was used to introduce modern infrastructure and amenities to resource-rich regions with the hope that these features would attract young workers and experts from the larger and over-populated cities of the Western, or European, USSR (2018). The city of Nurek, constructed to house the workers of a large dam built nearby, was constructed as a "city of the future." However, as Kalinovsky observes, there was considerable tension between these twin goals of resource extraction and city building. Conflict ensued between locals and newcomers as new industrial cities mirrored the problems of exclusivity seen in Central Asian capitals like Dushanbe, Tashkent, and Frunze. In these cities, where the dominant spoken language was Russian rather than Tajik, Uzbek, or Kyrgyz, local inhabitants of the region felt like outsiders (Kalinovsky 2018, 125). At the same time, Soviet planners began to view Central Asian cities as exemplars for the decolonizing world. As Kalinovsky writes, Khrushchev-era urban planning not only set out to facilitate resource mining, raise living standards, and spread urban development more evenly across the country; it also aimed to make "the Soviet Union a model for the postcolonial world" (2018, 118).

As "the largest city of the 'Soviet East'," Tashkent was a participant in the "global 1960s," becoming a hub for activities linking the USSR to newly independent decolonizing states in Asia and Africa (Kirasirova 2018; Eby 2021). As early as the 1950s, Tashkent International Radio broadcast global programming aimed at sharing information about Uzbek culture, industrialization, and urban development in the region (Stronski 2010, 240). In the 1960s, Tashkent hosted major international events, like the 1968 Tashkent International Afro-Asian Film Festival. As Masha Kirasirova writes, Tashkent's global status was "associated with the new [USSR]-wide search for legitimacy for Soviet power, and the reorientation of that search to 'the East.'" (2018). New architectural projects in Tashkent also served to demonstrate how Soviet modernist designs of this era could easily incorporate local, vernacular forms. New buildings like the Central State Museum of V. I. Lenin, opened in 1970, combined the horizontal modernist massing associated with Soviet public architecture of the period with Uzbek-inspired concrete geometric ornamentation stretching along the facade. The structure was designed by Russian architects working in partnership with Uzbek decorators (Figure 10; Kirasirova 2018).

The Soviet Union was not the only socialist country intent on exporting construction technology, along with socialist values, globally. In 1971, Erich Honecker, leader of GDR, initiated that country's *Wohnungsbauprogramm*, or

Figure 10 G. Rozanov, N. Shestopalov, and Iu. Boldychev, Tashkent Branch of the Museum of V.I. Lenin, 1970. Today, this building is the State Museum of the History of Uzbekistan. INTERFOTO / Alamy Stock Photo.

mass housing campaign. The goal of the campaign was the alleviate the GDR's housing crisis through the construction of *plattenbau*, or prefabricated concrete slab high-rises. As Annemarie Sammartino notes, with the intention of building one million new apartments for East German residents, planners leading the GDR's mass housing program drew inspiration from three sources: the USSR's microdistrict, the modernist Superblock, and American urban theorist Jane Jacobs (2018, 79). Similar East–West influences could also be found in the urban planning of the Yugoslav capital city of Belgrade, as Brigitte Le Normand shows (2014). Not long after undertaking its campaign to address the GDR's housing crisis, East German specialists traveled to the city of Vinh to aid in the process of rebuilding after a decade of US air strikes had destroyed much of this northern Vietnamese city. Among the sites constructed in Vinh by East German planners was the Quang Trong housing estate, consisting of nineteen housing blocks housing over 4,000 residents (Schwenkel 2020). As Christina Schwenkel notes, contributing to Vinh's reconstruction was at once part of a benevolent effort to spread socialist values and urbanism globally, while also serving as a way to engage a Cold War adversary. As Schwenkel writes, "solidarity was not motivated by altruism or anticolonialism alone, but also by national self-interest and conflict with West Germany as the GDR struggled to establish its political legitimacy" (2020, 83).

As Shin and Jung note, in rebuilding and expanding its urban housing stock after the Korean War, North Korea, a predominantly agrarian country prior to the war, relied on significant economic and material aid from the USSR and Eastern European socialist countries (2016). In cities across North Korea, microdistricts were constructed starting in the late 1950s following the Soviet model. Across areas of between fifteen to twenty-five hectares, new prefabricated four-to-five-story buildings were constructed in cities including Pyongyang, Hamhung, and Wonsan, a port city on the country's east coast (Figure 11). Between 1955 and 1962, East German planners also aided in the construction of housing districts in North Korea, though disagreements with DPRK officials and planners led to the reduction of East German aid to North Korea by as early as 1960 (Kim and Jung 2017). In the North Korean city of Hamhung, East German planners designed a model socialist city, introducing among other features the single-corridor-access apartment building. Apartment units, all accessed by a single corridor running along an external face of the building, were built in either one or two-room plans, though as Shin and Jung note, Kim Il Sung's preference for the two-room unit meant that this became the more popular for construction (Shin and Jung 2016). East German architects' work in Hamhung also led to schools becoming a "central factor in housing estate design" (Kim and Jung 2017).

Figure 11 Wonsan City, East Sea of Korea, Democratic People's Republic of Korea, North Korea.

In addition to competition in the realm of housing aid and development between capitalist and communist countries, communist powers also competed on this front with each other. In Mongolia's capital city in the 1960s, Soviet and Chinese architects vied for influence through the construction of rival residential districts. The Sino–Soviet split only raised the stakes of this competition. The rivalry played out on the outskirts of Ulaanbaatar, between the Soviet-designed and built twelfth microdistrict and the Chinese-designed and built fifth microdistrict. As Erofeev and Stanek note, the chief architect of Moscow was reportedly unimpressed by the quality of the Soviet district, compared to the superior quality of its Chinese counterpart (2021, 23). The Soviet Union would nonetheless continue to work actively in Mongolia, contributing individual buildings and other forms of building aid. In the early 1960s, the USSR donated a house-building factory to Mongolia. Built in Ulaanbaatar, this factory allowed Mongolia to produce for itself the prefabricated elements needed for the popular I-464 building system (Erofeev and Stanek 2021, 24).

The Soviet Union, China, and countries of the Eastern Bloc had much to gain from their interaction with the Global South. As Alessandro Iandolo notes, for Soviet leader Nikita Khrushchev, these relationships were part of a larger Cold War strategy to compete with the West "without war" (2012, 685). "Khrushchev's dream," he writes, "was as simple as it was visionary: once the developing world saw the full economic potential of socialism, it would turn its back on the capitalist and colonialist West and adopt socialism as a way of life. This would mean the final victory of state planning and production over free markets and private enterprise" (685). Socialist leaders' motivations for forging strong networks of exchange independent from capitalist networks naturally shifted over time. As Stanek writes, "by the 1970s, socialist countries were increasingly abandoning trade policies based on anti-imperialist solidarity, and they began to see the Global South as a reservoir of raw materials and mobile labor" (2020, 11). The next section will explore the continued globalization of the socialist city by turning to new geographies in Africa, Asia, and Latin America.

4 Decolonization and the Socialist City

By the early 1960s, Europe's overseas empires had largely collapsed in Asia and Africa and independent states formed in the place of former colonies. At this same moment, socialism gained new global reach, expanding dramatically with the collapse of European imperialism. Some postcolonial leaders, all too aware of the close ties between capitalism and empire, viewed socialism as a more promising path for development. For their part, Communist leaders in Eastern

Europe, the Soviet Union, and China packaged their approach to politics and economic planning for export, presenting socialism as a system with anti-imperialist roots dating back to the nineteenth century. Leaders like Josip Tito and Nikita Khrushchev worked directly to foster the spread of socialism by traveling to meet with African and Asian leaders, hosting them in turn in Belgrade and Moscow, and forging strong ties with the decolonial world through low-interest loans and technical assistance agreements. Chinese Premier Zhou Enlai visited Africa in 1964, touring ten newly independent African states in a bid to present an alternative model of revolutionary development, different from the Soviet, Yugoslav, and other East European varieties. As Jeremy Friedman observes, while the decolonizing world was "ripe for revolution," how to adapt socialism to suit the needs and conditions of newly independent Asian and African countries was an open question (2021, 1–5). In Latin America at this moment as well, socialism's appeal increased as that continent's revolutionary leaders looked for ways to counter US dominance. There too, different approaches to socialism were adopted. Far from there being a united communist movement working collectively toward global dominance, the years after 1945 saw the emergence of two major and at times rivaling socialist powers – the USSR and China – plus a growing number of smaller socialist states all of which vied with one another for influence in the decolonizing world.

In terms of its geographical and demographic reach, socialism spread widely in the second half of the twentieth century. By 1980, the socialist world encompassed one-third of the global population. And just as there was enormous variety in how socialism was adopted in different places, so too were there myriad global networks of exchange stretching across the socialist sphere. The global expansion of socialism in the second half of the twentieth century is a significant chapter in the history of globalization (Mark et al. 2020, 1–4). Recent scholarship shows that in architecture and urban planning, global socialist networks were robust (Stanek 2020). Vast new geographies of architectural knowledge production and exchange emerged with the expansion of socialism after 1945. Yet, as Łukasz Stanek notes in his pathbreaking study of networks linking Africa and the Middle East to Poland, Hungary, and other Eastern Bloc countries, "while Eastern European architects, planners, and construction companies are vividly remembered by professionals, inhabitants, and the general public in Ghana, Nigeria, Iraq, the United Arab Emirates, and Kuwait, their engagements in the Global South have been almost completely written out of the Western-based historiography of architecture" (2020, 2). The fall of socialism in Eastern Europe and the Soviet Union, the end of the Cold War, and the subsequent "triumph" of capitalism all but erased this history of socialist exchange, which is only now being recovered by a new generation of historians.

While in earlier sections we traced the expansion of socialism and the spread of socialist urbanism into Eastern Europe, Korea, China, Mongolia, and Vietnam after 1945, this section follows the further expansion of the socialist world starting in the 1950s into areas of Africa, Latin America, and new regions of Asia. In the second half of the twentieth century, socialist urbanism spread through global socialist networks and was forged often in reaction to the globalizing ambitions of capitalism. Diverse approaches to urban planning, and myriad urban experts, designs, and construction materials, traveled throughout these networks, resulting in similarities across socialist cities in an increasingly diverse range of geographical regions. Yet, key differences also emerged in cities across the socialist world as ideas and blueprints were either rejected or adapted and reworked to suit local preferences, needs, and conditions.

As the twentieth century progressed, socialist cities grew more connected while also becoming more varied. This section highlights some of the key divergencies, complexities, and breaks in the history of socialist urbanism. In their study of Soviet and Eastern European engagements with decolonization, James Mark and Paul Betts note that the new relationships and networks forged across the expanding socialist world after 1945 were neither easy nor straightforward. "There were always ambiguities and tensions," they write, "at the heart of these new relationships" (2022, 2). In some cases, these new connections reminded participants of earlier colonial relations. Tanzanian President Julius Nyerere saw East European and Soviet activities of the 1960s–1970s as a "Second Scramble for Africa" (Mark and Betts 2022, 3). Ultimately, the spread of socialist urbanism to new parts of the globe did not just see the duplication of Moscow, Warsaw, or Beijing's urban plans and architecture in cities like Dar es Salaam and Havana. Rather, the defining features of the socialist city evolved in response to its emergence in new locales.

Was socialism always synonymous with city building and urban life? This question is at the forefront of this section, because when we broaden geographically, following socialism through its global course in the second half of the twentieth century, the answer to this question is clearly no. While in the Soviet Union and Eastern Europe, socialist leaders located enormous revolutionary power in cities and in urban planning; this was not the case everywhere. When socialist and communist politics spread to new parts of the world in the second half of the twentieth century, revolutionary leaders came to view differently the relationship between cities and socialism. The dominant, revolutionary role attributed to cities by Soviet officials was not a view wholeheartedly embraced by leaders in China, as discussed in the previous section. Similarly, in the 1960s and 1970s, socialist and communist leaders in Vietnam, Cambodia, Cuba,

Tanzania and elsewhere expressed a skeptical, and at times hostile, view of the city. Were cities necessary for socialist revolutionary development? Why not focus on instilling and building revolutionary values in the countryside instead? In the decades after 1945, leaders like Tanzania's Julius Nyerere and Cuba's Fidel Castro actively worked to curb urbanization in their countries, focusing on the development of village and rural life. Aiming to keep urban centers small, socialist planners in these countries struggled against the primacy of capital cities like Dar es Salaam and Havana. This section, then, explores the development of socialist cities alongside the emergence of a socialist "antiurbanism," present to varying degrees in the decolonizing world in the second half of the twentieth century. That socialist life was not everywhere synonymous with urbanism and urbanization is an important development in the global effort to make cities socialist – one with implications for the global aspirations of the Soviet, East European, and Chinese urban models.

4.1 Socialist Antiurbanism in Cambodia

In the second half of the twentieth century, socialist city planning evolved as socialism and socialist urbanism spread to new regions of the world. New values came to be associated with cities and city life in the socialist world. As anthropologist Christina Schwenkel observes, "the relationship between cities and socialism was ambiguous and erratic, differing across time, space, and sphere of political influence" (2020, 29). While Vinh City, Schwenkel's focus, was rebuilt with the help of planners from the GDR in the 1970s, across the border in Cambodia communist leaders exacted intense violence on cities and urban inhabitants in the same period. The depopulation of the Cambodian capital of Phnom Penh by the Communist Party of Kampuchea, also known as the Khmer Rouge, during the Cambodian genocide of 1975–1979 serves as an extreme example of socialist antiurbanism, and even of "urbicide." The forced evacuation of Phnom Penh was carried out chaotically, taking a devastating toll and leading to the murder of tens of thousands of the city's residents (Kiernan 2008, 48–49). In language reminiscent of Stalin's Great Terror of the late 1930s and Mao's Great Leap Forward of 1958–62, Pol Pot's Khmer Rouge sought to "wipe clean" Cambodia by emptying out the country's cities and towns and "cleaning up and eliminating the filth of the rotten old society," as Radio Phnom Penh announced in May 1975 (McIntyre 1996, 730; Tyner et al. 2014, 1877).

As Tyner et al. argue, however, the long-held narrative that the Khmer Rouge "was guided by an antiurban bias" is incomplete (2014, 1873). Following Phnom Penh's depopulation, the city was repopulated and reopened, serving as "the catalytic center-point of Khmer Rouge policy and practice" (Tyner et al. 2014, 1874). The city's existing buildings and infrastructures either continued in their previous purposes or were reworked to suit the new regime. Single-family residences were transformed into communal dwellings and schools and other sites were turned into detention centers. As Phnom Penh's elites and intellectuals were executed or incarcerated, workers were forcibly brought back in to run the city's hospitals, garment factories, and warehouses (Tyner et al. 2014, 1887–1888). The Khmer Rouge relied on the capital city to accomplish its political goals.

Adding yet more nuance to this picture is the earlier history of architecture in socialist Phnom Pehn. From the time of Cambodian independence from France in 1953 until the anti-communist coup of 1970 and the civil war that followed, an era of "socialist-modernism" defined Phnom Pehn's postindependence redevelopment (Fauveaud 2020, 137). French-trained Cambodian architect Vann Molyvann and others, including numerous foreign architects, transformed the Cambodian capital through the construction of monumental spaces, like Phnom Pehn's wide new boulevards leading to the Independence Monument built in 1958 and like the city's new stadium, which would hold large political events. Later, in the late 1970s, the stadium would even host ceremonies staged by the Khmer Rouge (Fauveaud 2020, 141). The modernist Front du Bassac complex, completed in the 1960s with its waterfront apartments, theater, and communal spaces, similarly transformed the city. As Gabriel Fauveaud notes, these projects of the 1950s and 1960s together contributed to a New Khmer Architecture, which "was a symbiosis of the Modern Movement and Angkorian architecture of the classical period (twelfth-thirteenth centuries)" (2020, 139). This socialist-modernist postcolonial architectural heritage of the 1950s–1960s largely survived the violence of the Khmer Rouge, and it would continue to shape and define Phnom Penh into the 1990s and 2000s, as the country transitioned toward a market economy. While Cambodia under the Khmer Rouge offers us an extreme case of "socialist antiurbanism," the longer history of the country's postcolonial, socialist capital city opens to more complex narratives.

4.2 Cities and Socialism in East Africa

In 1966, five years after Tanzania achieved independence from Britain, a socialist drive-in movie theater opened in the capital city of Dar es Salaam, located on the Indian Ocean coast. In this city, with its population of just over a quarter million people, the theater drew huge crowds eager to watch foreign films imported from Hollywood, Bollywood, and elsewhere. Over the course of two decades, the drive-in cinema was a favorite spot in this cosmopolitan Tanzanian city for the collective pursuit of leisure. As historian Laura Fair argues, Dar's drive-in, a space beloved by the city's residents, was closely connected to the new Tanzanian state's socialist vision. The cinema "provided an architectural space where urban *ujamaa* and citizenship were given form" (2013, 1080). The drive-in theater offered a way for ordinary residents of the city to experience *ujamaa*, or African socialism, a term coined by Tanzanian President Julius Nyerere to separate his country's approach to socialism from Soviet, Chinese, and other models. As Fair writes, the drive-in was a symbol of the abundance offered by socialism, "bolstering claims that African socialism could provide the masses not just with goods, but with good times as well" (2013, 1079). As in the Soviet Union at the same moment, rates of private car ownership were rising among Tanzanian elites in the 1960s and 1970s, but one did not have to own a car to attend the drive-in cinema. Whether cinemagoers arrived on foot, by bus, or by car, the theater catered to all viewers, uniting them before the screen through the inclusion of mats and additional seating in front of the drive-in parking spaces. This was a space that brought together Tanzania's African and Asian residents. It was also a family affair, with Sundays quickly becoming the most popular day for all generations of the city's inhabitants to gather at the drive-in. This sense of unity continued into Monday morning, as cinemagoers discussed and debated the drama seen on the screen the night before. "Being able to contribute an informed analysis of the latest film was a hallmark of urban citizenship in Tanzania," Fair explains (2013, 1081).

Dar es Salaam's drive-in movie theater demonstrates some of the commonalities shared across socialist spaces, while also hinting at what made Tanzanian socialist urbanism unique. While Dar's drive-in was likely the world's only socialist *drive-in* cinema, films were an important and influential art form across the socialist world and movie theaters served as key spaces for socializing and socialization. As early as 1923, Soviet leader Leon Trotsky described the cinema as "the most important weapon [of collective education], a weapon excelling any other." In an article published in *Pravda*, titled "Vodka, the Church, and the Cinema," Trotsky argued that cinema was "the best instrument for propaganda, technical, educational, and industrial propaganda, propaganda against alcohol, propaganda for sanitation, political propaganda, any kind of propaganda you please, a propaganda which is accessible to everyone, which is attractive, which cuts into the memory and may be made a possible source of revenue." (Trotsky 1923) The drive-in cinema in Dar es Salaam did generate handsome profits for the Tanzanian state (Fair 2013, 1087), though it did not screen the kind of propaganda that Trotsky envisioned for Soviet audiences of the 1920s. Dar's drive-in served rather to forge a symbolic link between *ujamaa* and the urban good life, providing a coveted space for the pursuit of leisure. As David Crowley and Susan Reid observe in their work on socialist leisure in

Central and Eastern Europe, while state socialism is more typically associated with shortages, crumbling infrastructures, and state violence, pleasure was "integral to the utopian promise of communism, based as it was on notions of future abundance and fulfillment" (2010, 3).

Across the socialist world, urban spaces from the cinema to the concert hall to the street served as key sites of interaction and negotiation between the state and its citizens, especially youth. By the 1960s, popular culture was increasingly global, making "corrupting" Western influences difficult to stave off. In Tanzania, Western films were screened at the cinema in Dar es Salaam, but the country issued periodic bans on soul music and television (Ivaska 2002, 68). In examining youth culture in nearby Zanzibar, G. Thomas Burgess notes that competing influences could be found in public space during the socialist period. Revolutionary rhetoric promised victory in the people's battle against both colonialism and capitalism, but in everyday life aspects of Western consumer culture continued to shape Zanzibari youth. As in Dar es Salaam, Western films, for example, were screened in Zanzibar City in the 1960s and 1970s (Burgess 2002, 287). These films, Burgess notes, "paid no deference to socialist development or Islamic standards of decency and made no reference to the islands' historic race and class conflicts" (287). Instead, they presented an alternative vision of modern life – a vision that Zanzibari youth swiftly adopted. Bell bottoms and miniskirts became transgressive symbols signaling the wearer's disinterest and even dislike of revolutionary socialist development. Socialist leaders in Bulgaria would have found this familiar. There, the Communist Party that ruled from 1944 to 1989 fought the corrupting influence of "The Twist" and the Beatles. It sought to counter these youthful obsessions by mobilizing socialist leisure to "instill discipline and moral qualities into young people that would make them distinct from the 'passive' young generation living in capitalist societies" (Taylor 2006, 5). Youth culture may have seemed like an especially pressing concern in Bulgaria due to the high concentration of young people living in the country's cities. Youth exodus from the countryside meant that by 1975, 25 percent of the population of the capital city of Sofia were from the younger generation (46).

How to gain control over urban life and culture were problems facing socialist leaders around the world, but these issues took on new meaning in places undergoing decolonization. Not only were cities difficult to govern, in Africa and Asia many were also places built and shaped by colonial regimes, where colonial racial categories still governed the uses and perception of space (Callaci 2016). In Tanzania, the complexity of urban issues pushed that country's socialist leaders to turn increasingly away from the urban, seeing rural space as the primary location for the realization of *ujamaa.* In her work on city life in postcolonial Dar es Salaam, Emily Callaci shows that while the country's new socialist leaders initially viewed cities and their development as key to political liberation, they soon "sought to rein in this equation of liberation with urban modernization as Dar es Salaam swelled with migrants from the countryside and grew at a rate that far outpaced state capacity for urban planning, housing, and infrastructure" (2017, 18). In 1972, Nyerere made the decision to build a new capital city for Tanzania. Dodoma, located away from the Indian Ocean coast in the less populous center of the country, was envisioned as a "decolonized, authentically African modern city," or as Nyerere put it, "the chief village in the nation of villages" (Callaci 2016, 97–98). The new city's plan aimed to marry rural and urban. Residential areas, for example, were designed "in blocks of 10 family units surrounding a communal garden plot," a reference to village life (98). From downtown, the arable hills surrounding the city were visible. Ultimately, Dodoma never became the city that Nyerere envisioned. Despite careful planning, the city was plagued by informal settlement and its population never reached the 400,000 planned (Myers 2011; Callaci 2016). Yet, as Callaci writes, Tanzanian "leaders' projection of the African village as a model of modernity during a time of unprecedented urban growth was neither ironic nor contradictory, but rather strategic" (116). Pitting the blame for urban poverty and strife "squarely on the shoulders of urban Africans whose rightful place was in the village," Nyerere and other state officials deflected responsibility for the issues facing Tanzanian cities (116).

In neighboring Zanzibar, socialist leaders took a different approach to the city during the period of socialist development from 1964 and 1977. After achieving independence from Britain in December 1963, power over independent Zanzibar was quickly seized by members of the Marxist-Leninist African national Afro-Shirazi Party (ASP). Within a few months, ASP leaders agreed with Julius Nyerere on Articles of Union that united the islands of Zanzibar with mainland Tanganyika, creating the United Republic of Tanzania. As Garth Myers writes, although part of the same republic, the socialist development of Tanganyika and Zanzibar differ in important ways. The hallmarks of socialist development, for example, were implemented more swiftly in Zanzibar under the archipelago's socialist leader, Abeid Karume, than on the mainland overseen by Nyerere. Within just a year of its revolution, Zanzibar saw, for example, "the nationalization of land, confiscation and reallocation of the properties of the colonial era's elite, prohibition of all parties other than Karume's ASP, centralization of economic planning, and proclamation of socialist goals in urban policy" (Myers 2003, 108).

Karume was a leader keen to oversee major urban redevelopment projects directly. In a speech delivered in March 1964, he pledged to build a socialist

New Town in Zanzibar City (Folkers 2010, 80). Karume was also interested in mobilizing the resources available through global socialist networks to transform life in the island state. While the capitalist Federal Republic of Germany, or West Germany, was actively engaged in architectural development activities in mainland Tanzania, the GDR, or East Germany, eagerly established relations with Zanzibar (Wimmelbucker 2012, 408). This East–South relationship saw East German experts traveling to Zanzibar to offer advice and aid and Zanzibari students traveling to study in East Germany (Burgess 2021). In 1964, Karume invited East German urban planners to aid in the construction of new housing in Zanzibar City, which was to serve as a template for the later reorganization of the entire population of the islands "into ten new towns" (Myers 1994, 453). The global socialist interest in urban development efforts in the country also meant that by 1968, rival master plans for Zanzibar City were presented by the GDR and the People's Republic of China, which, like East Germany, saw relations with Zanzibar as a way to overcome its peripheral global status (Myers 1994, 452; Burgess 2021). Promising to modernize and "develop" the African country, East Germany secured strong ties with Karume's government, sending urban planners to contribute to the island's redevelopment in the late 1960s.

Shaped by centuries of colonial rule, Zanzibar City, located on the largest of Zanzibar's islands, grew by 60 percent in the decade between 1968 and 1978 (Myers 2003, 109). The city's Old Town, known as Stone Town, now a UNESCO heritage site, was home to most of the city's Arab, South Asian, and European residents. Along the waterfront of this elite district stood the House of Wonders, an imposing structure wrapped in wide verandahs affording maximum surveillance over the port city below. Built in the 1880s by Zanzibar's Omani sultan, who drew inspiration from an 1875 visit to England's Crystal Palace, the House of Wonders was designed by a German architect and was intended as a symbol of Zanzibar's cosmopolitan modernity. While the British, who dominated the island state from the 1890s, used the building as an administrative headquarters, Zanzibar's revolutionary socialist government transformed the structure into the ruling party's Ideological College (Myers 2003, 1–3). In addition to the House of Wonders, Stone Town was known for its parks, cinemas, cafes, and cool sea breezes (Burgess 2021). To the east of Stone Town, the newer district of Ng'ambo housed predominantly African residents. Residents of Ng'ambo, Swahili for "the other side," enjoyed far fewer amenities.

East German planners initially envisioned a planning solution that would not only help alleviate the city's housing shortage but would also address the spatial inequalities created by the city's segmented plan, inherited from the period of

British colonial rule. But this vision did not come to fruition. As Burgess writes, "if East Germany followed through on its promise to provide Africans with 'modern' housing it would rectify one of Zanzibar's most visible, galling, and visceral reminders of racial inequality" (Burgess 2021, 176). Instead, however, just two areas of Ng'ambo were selected for redevelopment. While nearly 7,000 new apartments were planned, just over 1,000 were built in large residential buildings assembled by forced, unpaid Zanzibari laborers (Myers 2003, 115; Wimmelbucker 2012, 424–427; Burgess 2021, 176). Today, Burgess notes, "the massive apartment blocks are stark reminders of the thousands of hours of forced labor required for their construction."

The socialist redevelopment of Zanzibar City was carried out more fully in propaganda than reality. As Garth Myers notes, the GDR's 1968 plan for the city "was accompanied by a propaganda blitz of posters, banners, and radio broadcasts designed to project its ideological vision of the cityscape" (2003, 112). Despite pronouncements emphasizing that the city's new residential development would bring about a new and improved way of life, Myers notes the considerable continuities in officials' approach to planning and governing the city from the colonial to revolutionary periods. Although the cityscape changed with the addition of East German *plattenbau*-style construction (Figure 12), older colonial spatial strategies persisted for policing, surveilling, and containing the city's population (Myers 2003, 114). Meanwhile, emptied of many of its elite residents

Figure 12 East German Plattenbau apartment blocks, Zanzibar, 2014. Joerg Boethling / Alamy Stock Photo.

who had fled the revolution, Stone Town was left to decay, resembling a ghost town, as one foreign journalist noted in 1966 (Burgess 2002, 292).

4.3 Socialist Cities in Cuba

In the years following the Cuban Revolution of 1959, Cuba's leaders similarly embraced an "antiurban position," choosing as Edge et al. write "to develop rural centers and provincial capitals rather than invest excessively in the national capital of Havana" (Edge et al. 2006, 90). Socialist Cuba's relationship with cities was shaped by the economic and social goals of the country's revolutionary leaders. Fidel Castro aimed to bring an end to Cuba's dependence on foreign capital, liberating the country from North American imperialism, as he put it in 1960 in his First Declaration of Havana. Diversifying and strengthening the island's agricultural output, heavily tilted toward the production of sugar for export, was key to this program of national liberation. These economic priorities had implications for urban development in the country. As Castro stated in 1966, the revolution would bring with it "a minimum of urbanism and a maximum of ruralism" (Cederlöf 2020, 54). The goal was to achieve territorial equity, elevating living standards not just in cities but in Cuba as a whole.

If Cuba's revolutionary leaders tended to view cities "as parasitic and corrupt places" (Scarpaci et al. 2002, 141), they nonetheless valued the role architects and urban planners would play in the country's struggle for national liberation. A younger generation of Cuban architects had been active in Castro's revolutionary movement prior to 1959. Many of them were committed Marxists, like Cuban architect Ricardo Porro, who participated in the revolutionary underground and was forced to flee to Venezuela in 1958 due to his involvement in revolutionary activities (Loomis 1999, 13). One year earlier, in 1957, the architecture student and revolutionary leader José Antonio Echeverría was killed in the failed Havana Presidential Palace attack. Like other socialist leaders, Castro saw Cuban architects as experts who would play a vital role in the country's path to socialism. Signaling the importance of the architectural profession, Fidel Castro himself paid a visit to Cuba's Colegio National de Arquitectos de Cuba (Cuban National College of Architecture) in February 1959, one month after taking power. Aiming to enlist Cuban architects in the revolutionary cause, Castro took to the floor at his meeting with the College to "proclaim an anti-capitalist sentiment and to stir the social consciousness of architects" (Braga 2017, 240). Cuba's new leader called on architects to support the revolution through new work on affordable housing construction that would serve all Cubans, not just the elites. Not all Cuban architects were on board with Castro's program. In fact, many of the country's most established figures quickly emigrated, leaving chaos in their wake in institutions like the National College, which was reorganized in 1959 and 1960 (Loomis 1999, 14).

Cuba's new focus on countering Havana's longstanding urban primacy by developing areas outside the capital and the revolutionary government's interest in housing contrasted sharply with the activities of the country's previous regime. Massive state and foreign investment in large-scale architectural projects in the capital characterized the final decade of rule of President Fulgencio Batista, the US-backed military dictator who governed Cuba until overthrown by Castro in 1959. In Batista's final years, Havanans witnessed in their city the construction of elite single-family homes in leafy bedroom communities and the erection of modernist high-rise office buildings in the city's central districts. American modernist architects from Wallace Harrison and Max Abramowitz to Philip Johnson built or planned major projects for Havana in this period (Loomis 1999, 6). Harrison and Abramowitz's US Embassy building, a glass and concrete high-rise constructed in 1952–1953, served as John Loomis writes as a "rather somber testimony to U.S. hegemony on the island" (9). The nearby Havana Hilton hotel and casino, one of President Batista's own pet projects, was completed one year before Batista was overthrown. Intended to help revive the Cuban economy through tourism, this twenty-five-story modernist glass and concrete building was seized by revolutionaries within months of opening. The hotel was nationalized and renamed the "Habana Libre" (the "Free Havana"). The building served as a headquarters for Castro's revolution. Later, it would host emissaries from socialist allies like the Soviet Union, which sent agricultural experts to visit the island to aid as advisors to their Cuban counterparts (Harmer 2019, 125).

Individual projects, like the Havana Hilton and the US Embassy, were pieces of a larger, unrealized plan for the redevelopment of Havana under Batista, a plan that threatened to demolish large swaths of Havana's historic districts, including the city's Old Town, rewriting the urban fabric of the city in modernist terms (Segre 2002, 209). In the 1950s, New York-based design firm Town Planning Associates, led by Josep Lluis Sert, Paul Lester Wiener, and Paul Schulz, was invited to implement the Master Plan for Havana. As architectural historian Roberto Segre writes, this plan drew inspiration from the Athens Charter, cleaving to principles elaborated in the interwar years by members of Congrès Internationaux d'Architecture Moderne (CIAM), including the "thesis on the separation of functions (*zoning*) and the predominance of empty spaces in the central areas" (209). Taking automobile traffic as a primary concern, Sert and associates envisioned a reworked city center, with widened streets and the centers of blocks "vacated" for parking (Plan for Havana, 10). Segre, who credited the revolution of 1959 for saving Havana's historic Old Town from destruction, noted in 2002 that "the hope of achieving a metropolis with three million inhabitants – in a country of six million in the 1950s – was a utopia which was totally removed from the reality of an island characterized by underdevelopment and prevailing poverty in the greater part of its territory. It was the illusion of forming a city destined for North American tourism, integrated with the Miami-Las Vegas axis . . . " (Segre, 209). Following the Cuban Revolution of 1959, Havana and other cities on the island would form alternative axes with cities of the socialist world. Sert, meanwhile, would direct his attention to his US Embassy in Baghdad, completed in 1961. While Cuba's new revolutionary government shifted focus from urban to rural affairs, Iraqi officials following the 14 July Revolution in 1958 prioritized industry, housing, and public buildings over rural development, attracting a flurry of investment from both the capitalist and socialist world (Stanek 2020, 176).

Despite the Cuban revolutionary state's focus on rural development, Havanans would see transformations to their city with the arrival of socialism. Residents of Havana found protection in new laws halting evictions and mandating the lowering of rents or, in the case of those living in tenements, the elimination of rent entirely (Scarpaci et al. 2002, 131, 134). As in Moscow after the Bolshevik Revolution, Havana's elite properties, like those in the city's Miramar neighborhood, were seized from owners and put to new public use after 1959. In Miramar, expropriated mansions were transformed into "schools and dormitories for thousands of children on scholarships who marched in orderly lines along Fifth Avenue, imitating the marches by the light-blue-shirted worker militias" (Scarpaci et al. 2002, 131). Along that same Fifth Avenue in the late 1970s, construction began on the Soviet Embassy. This playful constructivist building, designed by Soviet architects Aleksandr Rochegov and Mariia Engel'ke, rivaled the US Embassy built in the unadorned International Style. Soviet and broader socialist influence could be seen elsewhere too, in prefabricated housing blocks that began to rise on Havana's cityscape in the decades after the revolution. New public spaces emerged in socialist Havana as well, made possible by the nationalization of private businesses and property. These spaces, like Parque Coppelia that opened in 1966, served both as informal gathering places and as ideologically infused locales communicating to residents the mores and aspirations of the new regime.

The leafy green foliage of Havana's Parque Coppelia continues today to offer shade for visitors of the park's main attraction: the Coppelia ice cream parlor. The modernist structure of the parlor and its surrounding landscape represent a fusion of vernacular and socialist design. Built on a raised platform at the heart of the park, the parlor is a two-story modernist circular building constructed from lightweight concrete. The parlor serves Cuba's internationally acclaimed Coppelia ice cream, first produced in the 1960s in response to US trade embargoes. The park surrounding the parlor, as James Curtis writes, "evokes elements of the traditional Latin American plaza" while also showing how "socialist ideology and orientations help shape the design and use of public spaces" (62). The park was designed, Curtis notes, to encourage circulation and interaction among those who visit, sit for a time, and pass through. The space serves as "a public space, town square, and point of encounter for what used to be commonly referred to as the revolution's *hombre integrado* (new integrated person)" (Scarpaci et al. 2002, 305).

One of socialist Havana's premiere architectural projects undertaken shortly after the revolution, the Escuelas Nacionales de Arte (National Art Schools), reflected the new opportunities available in public architectural projects for exploring Cuban national themes and identities (Edge et al. 2006). Built between 1961 and 1965 on the site a former golf course confiscated after the revolution, the Art Schools capture in architectural form the search for *cubanidad* – a distinctly Cuban style, or Cubanness (Loomis 1999). A cultural debate with roots in Cuba's late-nineteenth-century movement for independence from Spain, *cubanidad* took on new meaning in the revolutionary period. The Art Schools was designed by the Cuban architect Ricardo Porro, who in 1960 returned to Cuba from exile in Venezuela, and by Italian architects Roberto Gottardi and Vittorio Garatti. Porro, who joined the faculty at Cuba's National School of Architecture upon his return following the revolution, sought to capture in his design for the Art Schools a distinctly Cuban style, drawing inspiration from Afro-Cuban culture. In response to the US economic blockade, imposed in 1960, and in keeping with the spirit of the project, the design for the schools eschewed materials like steel and Portland cement, making use instead of local, earthen materials like brick and terra-cotta tile (Loomis 1999, 25). In both form and function, the Art Schools stood as a rejection of the universalizing International Style that predominated in large projects undertaken in Havana by American architects before 1959, like the Havana Hilton (1958) and the US Embassy (1953).

Just five years after Cuba's revolution, the country's socialist leaders articulated a vision for Havana with the adoption of the city's first socialist master plan of 1963–1964. The master plan aimed to reduce the density of central Havana, then a city of about 1.5 million residents. It put in place measures to address environmental concerns by rerouting maritime traffic in the Havana Harbor and by decreasing the number of industrial and garbage disposal sites located within the city. The plan also aimed to address the city's housing crisis.

Inspired by principles earlier elaborated by CIAM and in Soviet urban planning, the Havana master plan reimagined the spatial organization of the city, grouping residential zones into microdistricts, districts, and regions and calling for new housing construction (Scarpaci et al. 2002, 152–155). Finally, Havana's first master plan established an interconnected system of parks, that included a Botanical Garden, a National Zoo, and a Lenin Park. This urban park system would link up to an outlying agricultural greenbelt, developed to feed the entire city, or so the plan's authors hoped.

The Havana Greenbelt was an ambitious program that was never fully realized. It aimed to make the city of Havana self-sufficient, by growing food for the capital in successive belts of fruit trees, coffee cultivation, and dairy pastures (Diaz and Harris 2005, 141). Cuban officials never reached their ambitious plan of intensifying agricultural production across a full 10,000 hectares of agricultural land circling Havana. But the Havana Greenbelt did see significant agricultural development around the city, as well as the construction of prefabricated housing for farmers. The Greenbelt had the further effect of temporarily transforming Havanans into a rural labor force – a model duplicated at the time in other areas of Cuba (Scarpaci et al. 2002, 140). As Scarpaci et al. write, "administrators, technicians, workers, housewives, and students dressed in rural workers' clothes would leave Havana to work in the countryside" (140). The Havana Greenbelt helped to give this city a sharply delineated boundary between urban and rural zones, a feature that continued to define Havana into the twenty-first century (Hirt and Scarpaci 2007). Even so, Havana's sharp urban edge could easily soften in everyday practice, as the experience of the city's administrators-turned-farmers indicates.

Cuba has been intensely shaped by its geographical proximity to the United States. The country's socialist urban policies have reflected concerns about American dominance, with socialist leaders' antiurbanism spurred in part by a desire to develop self-sufficiency in agriculture and other areas. The port city of Cienfuegos, located on the south coast of the island, was developed extensively in the 1970s and 1980s to house large-scale energy infrastructural facilities designed to power and protect the island. The construction of a Czechoslovak electricity plant and a Soviet oil refinery propelled the growth and development of the city, shaped in earlier centuries by its role as a colonial shipping hub in the Caribbean sugar economy. In 1960, Cuba's revolutionary government began exporting sugar once again, now through the port city's new bulk sugar terminal, opened in 1967, and this time to a new trade partner: the Soviet Union. In exchange, Soviet oil and consumer goods flowed into Cuba through Cienfuegos (Cederlöf 2020, 61–62). As Gustav Cederlöf argues, Cienfuegos "should be understood relationally," as a space produced through its ties with the world beyond Cuban borders (2020, 54). Cuba's participation in networks that bound the socialist world was on display not just in Cienfuegos's oil refinery that processed Soviet crude oil or the "Carlos Marx" cement factory imported from the GDR and built just outside the city. These global ties could also be seen in Cienfuegos's new Ciudad Nuclear, or Nuclear City.

In 1983, construction began on the Bay of Cienfuegos on one of four nuclear reactors that were to make up Cuba's Juragua power plant, dubbed "The Project of the Century" by the Cuban government. Part of a larger effort to generate enough electricity through nuclear power to sustain the island, the power plant near Cienfuegos was a testament to the promise and ambition of socialist development. As Cederlöf writes, "the nuclear plant would develop the country's productive forces in one leap, thrusting Cuba onto a higher stage of techno-material development" (66). The Nuclear City built to the east of the power plant carried this same utopian promise. The city, set along two parallel avenues, was built up with five-story prefabricated structures constructed using the IMS Žeželj system, invented in 1957 in socialist Yugoslavia (Cederlöf 2020, 72; Jovanovic 2021, 311). The Nuclear City's IMS housing blocks, outfitted with nearby amenities including a library, post office, and clinic, connected Cuban residents to a global experience of socialist urbanism. Not only did Cubans living in Cienfuegos's Nuclear City live side by side with Bulgarian and Soviet engineers, they also lived in housing common in countries from Hungary and China to Ethiopia and Angola (Cederlöf 2020, 72; Jovanovic 2021, 311).

The future of Cuba's Nuclear City was tied to the fate of global socialism. The Chornobyl (Chernobyl) disaster of 1986 drew increased scrutiny of Cuba's nuclear ambitions from this country's neighbors, most notably from the United States. And the fall of the USSR in 1991 brought an end to the supply of crude oil to Cuba, precipitating a long period of decline and decay for the country and its still-incomplete Nuclear City. The history of socialist cities in Cuba is set firmly against the backdrop of the Cold War, a subject we examine next in greater detail.

5 The Cold War and the Socialist City

The Cold War and the emergence after 1945 of two global superpowers – the United States and the USSR – intensified the competition between socialist and capitalist urbanism. After 1945 and until the early 1990s, the world was divided into communist and capitalist camps. The Cold War, fought through proxy wars like those in Korea, Vietnam, and Afghanistan, was also fought on the ideological, cultural, and architectural fronts. Architects, urban planners, and state leaders used rival urban planning philosophies as tools in this conflict that simmered for over four decades. The rivalry that emerged during the Cold War between capitalist and socialist cities and city builders had significant effects on urban development in the socialist world.

At the forefront of world cities most fundamentally transformed by the Cold War is Berlin. After the defeat of Nazi Germany in 1945, Berlin was divided into sectors overseen initially by the four Allied powers, the United States, France, Britain, and the USSR. When Cold War tensions rose in the late 1940s between the Western powers and the Soviet Union, these divisions became permanent features of the city. Starting in 1950, an internal border zone was established, creating a West and an East Berlin. This was followed in 1961 by the construction of the Berlin Wall. Dividing the city until residents tore it down in 1989, the wall became a symbol of the vast gulf that opened after 1945 between the East and the West, communism and capitalism. This symbol built on an earlier one: the "iron curtain," a term coined by Winston Churchill in a speech in 1946. These symbols are useful in helping to understand the tenor of the Cold War era that stretched from the years immediately after 1945 to the fall of the Soviet Union in 1991. Yet, they misleadingly suggest that there was little to no contact between the East and the West during this period. In the sphere of urbanism and city development, this was simply not the case.

5.1 International Encounters between Urban Experts across the Cold War Divide

Like experts in other fields, urban specialists encountered one another at conferences, meetings, and events that united professional communities across the Cold War divide. The twentieth century saw the internationalization of the architectural and planning professions. The century witnessed the creation of new international institutions like the Pan-American Congress of Architects, which held its first meeting in 1920, in the wake of a first world war, and the International Union of Architects, which met first in 1948 in yet another postwar era. The Cold War drove a wedge between urban professionals working in capitalist and communist countries – experts who, in the case of those hailing from the Allied nations, had set aside ideological differences during the war to work together against a common enemy (Cohen 2011). But international activities bringing together experts from both the East and the West continued into the Cold War era. Rather than halting international activity, the Cold War generated new forms of global engagement, with urban design and architecture becoming an important front for direct Cold War competition.

In 1960, architects from the Americas gathered for the Tenth Pan-American Congress of Architects, taking place that year in Buenos Aires. Held shortly after the Cuban Revolution, this congress served as a site for early interactions between experts working across the new socialist–capitalist divide that was just emerging at this moment in the Americas. At the event, Cuban architects sought to broadcast their country's new socialist mantras and mandates, in the hopes that other countries in the region would follow suit. Cubans' continued engagement in Pan-American institutions after 1959 helped to spread socialist ideas about architecture and urbanism in the region, at once inspiring and vexing international colleagues. Architects from the United States in attendance at the Pan-American Congress of 1960 would report back to Washington, DC on their Cuban colleagues' activities and behaviors. Believing the Cuban delegates to have been "coached by Moscow," the US architects took the socialist presence at the Pan-American Congress of Architects as an indication of Soviet orchestration of the "social unrest prevailing in several of the member countries."[6] The 1960s, punctuated by dramatic Cold War incidents like the Cuban Missile Crisis of 1962, would see tensions mount further between the communist and capitalist architectural camps.

Three years after the Buenos Aires congress, in 1963, Cuba hosted the International Union of Architects (UIA) Congress in Havana. The location for this event, which centered on the theme "Architecture in Developing Countries," was chosen prior to the Cuban Revolution. Receiving assurances from Castro, UIA organizers decided to go ahead, even as US-based architects pledged to boycott the event. (As a compromise, a second, smaller UIA gathering was held in October 1963 in Mexico City.) UIA delegates from Western Europe did attend the main congress, arriving in Havana in September 1963 on a chartered flight from Paris, since commercial flights no longer operated from Western European cities following the revolution (International Union of Architects 1998, 113). Altogether, 1,200 delegates representing 69 countries attended the Havana event. Provocatively, Cuban architects opted to hold as part of the proceedings an international design competition for a monument commemorating the "Victory of Playa Girón in the Bahia de Cochinos." This Bay of Pigs monument competition was won by Polish architects, with Brazilian and Bulgarian submissions tying for second, and a Soviet submission receiving third place (Glendinning 2009, 208, 211, 216).

This was not the first time that one of the UIA's congresses was held in a socialist country. In 1958, the fifth UIA Congress was held in Moscow.

6 Report from Samuel Inman Cooper to the Board of Directors of the American Institute of Architects on the X Pan-American Congress of Architects, January 1961, Henry S. Churchill Papers, Cornell University Library, collection 2347, box 1, folder 4.

The UIA was founded after WWII to bring together architects for global discussions on the world's most pressing issues in architecture and urban planning. Despite the perennial controversies plaguing its work, the UIA continued its activities through the Cold War era. As Miles Glendinning observes, despite its small size and peripheral position outside more influential modernist circles, the UIA managed to secure for itself an outsized role in international architectural relations. As he argues, the UIA "was able to exploit the polarisations of the Cold War to carve out an influential mediating niche for itself" (2009, 198). Events like those organized by the UIA were crucial sites of exchange and encounter for architects and planners working across the East and the West. While urban experts convened at international meetings, ordinary urbanites also encountered one another, albeit in different ways, across the Cold War divide.

5.2 International Encounters between Socialist and Capitalist Urbanites

From late July to early September 1959, millions of Soviet citizens visited Moscow's Sokolniki Park. While some of those visitors no doubt went to the popular urban park simply to stroll the grounds of what was once a royal falconry forest, most of the tens of thousands who visited that summer went to see the American National Exhibition. Curated by the United States Information Agency, the American National Exhibition occupied a small section of the expansive urban greenspace in Moscow's northeast, but it drew huge crowds of curious Soviet citizens eager to catch a glimpse of "ordinary" American life. The American National Exhibition, the site of the famous and impromptu "Kitchen Debate" between Khrushchev and Nixon, was held in Moscow at the height of the Cold War and it demonstrated how the world's two superpowers, the United States and the USSR, sought to compete with one another in the cultural arena. In June 1959 in New York City, the USSR mounted its own exhibition, displaying for Americans the latest achievements in Cold War technology, from Soviet rockets and satellites to nuclear power. A model of Sputnik, the first artificial satellite that the USSR proudly launched into earth's low orbit in 1957, dangled from the ceiling of New York's Coliseum convention center. For their exhibition in Moscow, the Americans countered with a different approach, aiming as Greg Castillo writes "to shift the terms of the debate from military hardware to modern housewares – a domain of uncontested American preeminence" (2010, viii). The USSR may have been winning the space race, but Americans had consumerism clinched. In these dueling exhibitions held in Moscow and New York City in 1959, the world's two superpowers competed for supremacy, vying for dominance in the cultural sphere.

When then Vice President Richard Nixon opened the American National Exhibition in Moscow in July 1959 with a ribbon-cutting ceremony attended by Soviet leader Nikita Khrushchev, the future US President was engaging in a larger American effort to fight the Soviet Union using "soft power." This realm of Cold War competition is sometimes referred to as the "Nylon War," a term coined by sociologist David Riesman in 1951. As Susan Reid explains, "the most powerful missiles in Riesman's conception of nylon warfare were consumer items (such as vacuum cleaners and beauty aids) that were targeted at women" (2009, 87). In the case of the American National Exhibition, the publicly stated goal on the American side was to promote "mutual understanding" and to inform the Soviet public about the nature of America. Internally, however, US Information Agency staff also discussed a second goal: "to reorient Soviet citizens' individual desires in a direction that would corrode their state" (Turner 2013, 247). The Americans curating this exhibit worked on the assumption that Soviet citizens, accustomed to routine shortages of consumer goods in their own country, would be deeply impressed by the range and quality of goods available to the average American – so impressed that they might even lose faith in their government or destabilize it by demanding greater attention to the consumer economy. The Americans planning this exhibit for Moscow also believed that there was an intrinsic connection between democracy and capitalism that fueled the American suburban lifestyle: as Fred Turner writes, the democratic person, they thought, was someone with the freedom to choose, not only from a "slate of political leaders, but from a range of consumer goods" (Turner 2013, 215).

In unveiling the exhibition in Moscow in 1959, Nixon thus threw open a door in the Soviet capital to the highly exciting and enticing world of American suburban life. American cars, a model supermarket, the latest home gadgets and consumer goods, and fully furnished model homes were all on display at the exhibition. The exhibit was structured not just to entice Soviet visitors, but to surveil them. Bilingual English-Russian speaking guides were out on the floor to answer visitors' questions. Later, these guides would be debriefed, collecting in their reports data on the "mood" of the Soviet visitors. An early IBM computer on the floor of the exhibit allowed visitors to walk up and ask questions about the United States, spitting preprogrammed replies and recording the precise questions posed by Soviet people. And finally, there were comment books out on the floor ready to capture Soviet reactions directly.

With American daily life so nicely packaged for Soviet consumption, how did Soviet citizens respond? The American National Exhibition left a powerful impression on Soviet visitors to the show during that summer of 1959. As one Soviet visitor commented, "Leaving the exhibition, I carry with me an impression of glittering metal saucepans." "Okay, Yankees!" another exclaimed, "Some day we will catch up with you in all areas where we lag behind. But in general we wish you well and would like to hear the same from you addressed to us." Others responded less generously. A group of visitors noted that "we think that a country which has existed without wars and destruction for about two centuries could show greater achievements in technology, science, culture and even everyday living." Another visitor asked, disappointedly, "Is it possible that you think our mental outlook is restricted to everyday living only?"[7]

Soviet visitors responded with a mix of admiration, envy, denial, and indifference. An important theme in Soviet responses, both from visitors to the exhibit and from Soviet officials, related to the theme of improving the lives of women. While the United States claimed to be improving women's lives through the production of technologically advanced kitchens, Soviet officials and planners responded by pointing to the smaller and more efficient kitchen spaces then being produced in the USSR's new mass-produced prefabricated apartment blocks. Still, as Susan Reid notes, Soviet officials knew that in the allocation of domestic comforts and consumer goods, they had work to do to catch up to the United States. As Reid writes, "after the exhibition (although not solely in response to it), further measures to increase output of consumer goods (especially domestic appliances) were announced" (2009, 105). Khrushchev's mass housing campaign was already underway and there was increased demand among Soviet citizens for better, more affordable furniture and domestic goods. At the very same moment that many Americans were moving out to new homes in the suburbs, Soviet families were moving into new single-family apartments in microdistricts located on the outskirts of socialist cities.

6 The Afterlives of Socialist Cities

In 2012, André Kuipers, an astronaut working for the European Space Agency, photographed Berlin from space. Taken from the International Space Station, this image captures the once-divided city of Berlin illuminated at night. Incredibly, the astronaut's photograph, taken over twenty years after the reunification of Berlin, still shows evidence of the city's former divide. The Space Station's Nightpod camera was sharp enough to capture differences across the city's streetlight infrastructure: the whiter light of West Berlin contrasted clearly with the yellower hue of East Berlin's streetlights. Communist states collapsed

[7] "Comments on Exhibition" in *The Kitchen Debate and Cold War Consumer Politics: A Brief History with Documents*, ed. By Shane Hamilton and Sarah T. Phillips, (Boston: Bedford, 2014), 64–66.

in Europe between 1989 and 1991, but socialist cities in this region did not simply transform into capitalist cities overnight. Long after the fall of the Berlin Wall and long after the dissolution of the Soviet Union, remnants of the socialist city remain in these places, as they do elsewhere in the once-socialist and still-socialist world. While political and economic systems can change rapidly, cities and their material infrastructures are much more enduring.

This Element has argued that socialist cities were global by design; that they transformed relations in the twentieth century between citizens and the state; and that they were forged through competition (and at times collaboration) with the capitalist world as well as by ever-expanding socialist urban networks. Urbanites of the twentieth century witnessed both the socialist reconstruction of existing urban spaces like Zanzibar and Beijing and the creation of entirely new socialist cities like Nowa Huta and Cienfuegos. Having examined socialist cities comparatively and interrelationally, what are we to make of the "after-lives" of socialist cities? What happens to a socialist city once it no longer exists within a socialist state? This question has animated a generation of scholars concerned with post-socialist transition.

In examining the afterlives of socialist cities, scholars working across disciplines have explored what it means for residents of these spaces today that the built environment of the past holds firm, continuing to shape and structure the present. This is not to say that the flow of capitalism into formerly and still-socialist regions has not registered spatial change. In her book *Iron Curtains*, Sonia Hirt examines the gates, suburbs, and urban enclosures that began to appear in Sofia, Bulgaria in the 1990s (2012). The privatization of institutions, housing, and infrastructure under capitalism has opened the door to fundamentally new experiences in cities. The urban spaces of the former Soviet Union and Eastern Europe have changed over the past few decades in dramatic and noticeable ways. The immediate post-socialist period saw socialist urban plans discredited along with the regimes that implemented them. Symbolic city spaces were among the first to fall as residents and new post-socialist officials took charge.

In some cities, socialist monuments have been toppled. In others, monuments have been defaced. Bulgaria's Monument to the Red Army, built in Sofia in 1954, was transformed in the 1990s into a canvas for an ever-evolving visual protest; paint recasts the monument's statuary as pop culture icons that shift over time, from Ronald McDonald to Wonder Woman. More recently, this monument has been painted in blue and yellow in honor of independent Ukraine. In Nowa Huta, a temporary neon yellow Lenin statue was erected in 2014, titled "Fountain of the Future." The new Lenin was a twist on the city's earlier socialist-era monument: instead of gesturing toward the "bright communist future," the first Soviet leader is shown with his pants down, urinating (Cascone 2014).

Since the fall of socialism in Eastern Europe and the former Soviet Union, socialist city spaces have been converted, subverted, disfigured, and destroyed. And yet, across this region, socialist urbanism continues to stubbornly shape everyday life and to determine and hamstring many post-socialist planning decisions. Kimberly Zarecor argues that "the socialist city as a type is not bounded by the beginning or end of the socialist regime, but rather can be defined as a stage of urban development with a recognizable set of priorities for decision-making" (2018, 96–97). The socialist city continues to exist today, Zarecor argues, through the public transportation networks, green spaces, public utility systems, and housing developments that were built during the socialist period. And as Stephen Collier (2011) and Jane Zavisca (2012) show, these infrastructures doggedly resist the neoliberal projects and plans of the post-socialist era. Post-socialist cities are deeply shaped by what Erofeev and Stanek call the "path-dependencies of socialist urbanism" (2021, 45). This includes socialist-era water, waste, and transportation infrastructures, as well as urban experts' own past experiences, memories, habits, and training.

It is worth saying that socialism is not dead. Today, new chapters in the history of the socialist city are being written. In states that still consider themselves socialist, from China and North Korea to Cuba, building socialist cities is not just a phenomenon of the past. We might now ask how theories and plans for socialist cities have changed, now that large parts of the world are no longer socialist. Socialist urbanism was and is influential beyond "actually existing" socialist cities. Socialist mayors and mayoral candidates have in recent years introduced or advocated for socialist policies, plans, and visions in American cities like Seattle and Buffalo. Architects and planners carried socialist ideas into their designs for capitalist cities. Whether in post-socialist spaces, still existing socialist cities, or in parts of the world never ruled by state socialism, the long history of socialist urbanism remains influential.

References

Anderson, Richard. 2015. *Russia: Modern Architectures in History*. London: Reaktion.

Andrusz, Gregory, Michael Harloe and Ivan Szelenyi. 1996. *Cities after Socialism: Urban and Regional Change and Conflict in Post-Socialist Societies*. Cambridge, MA: Blackwell Publishers.

Barenberg, Alan. 2014. *Gulag Town, Company Town: Forced Labor and Its Legacy in Vorkuta*. New Haven: Yale University Press.

Bater, James H. 1980. *The Soviet City*. Beverly Hills: Sage Publications.

Betts, Paul, and James Mark. 2022. *Socialism Goes Global: The Soviet Union and Eastern Europe in the Age of Decolonisation*. Oxford: Oxford University Press.

Beyer, Elke. 2012. Competitive Coexistence: Soviet Town Planning and Housing Projects in Kabul in the 1960s. *The Journal of Architecture* 17 (3): 309–332.

Bocharnikova, Daria. 2014. *Inventing Socialist Modern: A History of the Architectural Profession in the USSR, 1954–1971*. PhD dissertation, European University Institute Florence.

Bocharnikova, Daria, and Steven E Harris. 2018. Second World Urbanity: Infrastructures of Utopia and Really Existing Socialism. *Journal of Urban History Journal of Urban History* 44 (1): 3–8.

Bray, David. 2005. *Social Space and Governance in Urban China: The Danwei System from Origins to Reform*. Palo Alto: Stanford University Press.

Braga, Patrick Calmon de Carvalho. 2017. Arquitectura Cuba and the Early Revolutionary Project. *International Journal of Cuban Studies* 9 (2): 235–259.

Burgess, Thomas. 2002. Cinema, Bell Bottoms, and Miniskirts: Struggles over Youth and Citizenship in Revolutionary Zanzibar. *The International Journal of African Historical Studies* 35 (2/3): 287–313.

Burgess, Thomas. 2021. The Rise and Fall of a Socialist Future: Ambivalent Encounters between Zanzibar and East Germany in the Cold War. In *Navigating Socialist Encounters: Moorings and (Dis)Entanglements between Africa and East Germany during the Cold War*, 169–192. Edited by Eric Burton, Anne Dietrich, Immanuel R. Harisch, and Marcia C. Schenck. Oldenbourg: De Gruyter.

Callaci, Emily. 2016. "Chief Village in a Nation of Villages": History, Race and Authority in Tanzania's Dodoma Plan. *Urban History* 43 (1): 96–116.

2017. *Street Archives and City Life: Popular Intellectuals in Postcolonial Tanzania*. Durham: Duke University Press.

Cascone, Sarah. June 16, 2014. New Polish Fountain Portrays a Peeing Vladimir Lenin. *Artnet News*. https://news.artnet.com/art-world/new-polish-fountain-portrays-a-peeing-vladimir-lenin-40816

Castillo, Greg. 1994. Moscow: Gorki Street and the Design of the Stalin Revolution. In *Streets: Critical Perspectives on Public Space*, 57–70. Edited by Zeynep Celik, Diane Favro, and Richard Ingersoll. Berkeley: University of California Press.

1997a. Peoples at an Exhibition: Soviet Architecture and the National Question. In *Socialist Realism Without Shores*, 91–119. Edited by Thomas Lahusen and Evgeny Dobrenko. Durham and London: Duke University Press.

1997b. Soviet Orientalism: Socialist Realism and Built Tradition. *Traditional Dwellings and Settlements Review* 8 (2): 33–47.

2010. *Cold War on the Home Front: The Soft Power of Midcentury Design*. Minneapolis: University of Minnesota Press.

Cederlöf, Gustav. 2020. The Revolutionary City: Socialist Urbanisation and Nuclear Modernity in Cienfuegos, Cuba. *Journal of Latin American Studies* 52 (1): 53–76.

Chan, Kam Wing, and Will Buckingham. 2008. Is China Abolishing the Hukou System? *The China Quarterly* (195): 582–606.

Clark, Katerina. 2000/1981. *The Soviet Novel: History as Ritual*. Bloomington: Indiana University Press.

Cohen, Jean-Louis. 2011. *Architecture in Uniform: Designing and Building for the Second World War*. New Haven: Yale University Press and the Canadian Centre for Architecture.

Collier, Stephen. 2011. *Post-Soviet Social: Neoliberalism, Social Modernity, Biopolitics*. Princeton: Princeton University Press.

Conterio, Johanna. 2022. Controlling Land, Controlling People: Urban Greening and the Territorial Turn in Theories of Urban Planning in the Soviet Union, 1931–1932. *Journal of Urban History* 48 (3): 479–503.

Cooke, Catherine. 1978. Russian Responses to the Garden City Idea. *Architectural Review* 163: 353–363.

Crawford, Christina E. 2022. *Spatial Revolution: Architecture and Planning in the Early Soviet Union*. Ithaca: Cornell University Press.

Crowley, David. 2003. *Warsaw*. London: Reaktion Books.

Crowley, David, and Susan Reid. 2010. Introduction: Pleasures in Socialism? In *Pleasures in Socialism: Leisure and Luxury in the Eastern Bloc*, 3–51. Edited by Crowley and Reid. Evanston: Northwestern University Press.

Crowley, David, and Susan E. Reid, eds. 2002. *Socialist Spaces: Sites of Everyday Life in the Eastern Bloc*. 1st ed. New York: Berg Publishers.

David-Fox, Michael. 2012. *Showcasing the Great Experiment: Cultural Diplomacy and Western Visitors to the Soviet Union, 1921–1941*. Oxford: Oxford University Press.

DeHaan, Heather. 2013. *Stalinist City Planning: Professionals, Performance, and Power*. Toronto: University of Toronto Press.

Díaz, Jorge Peña, and Phil Harris. 2005. Urban Agriculture in Havana: Opportunities for the Future. In *Continuous Productive Urban Landscapes*. London: Routledge.

Dobczansky, Markian. 2016. From Soviet Heartland to Ukrainian Borderland: Searching for Identity in Kharkiv, 1943–2004. PhD dissertation, Stanford University.

Dyak, Sofia. 2023. From War into the Future: Historical Legacies and Questions for Postwar Reconstruction in Ukraine. *Architectural Histories* 11(1): 1–11.

Eby, Marek. 2021. Global Tashkent: Transnational Visions of a Soviet City in the Postcolonial World, 1953–1966. *Ab Imperio* 4: 238–264.

Edge, K., J. Scarpaci, and H. Woofter. 2006. Mapping and Designing Havana: Republican, Socialist and Global Spaces. *JCIT Cities* 23 (2): 85–98.

Emeliantseva, Ekaterina. 2011. The Privilege of Seclusion: Consumption Strategies in the Closed City of Severodvinsk. *Ab Imperio* 2: 238–259.

Erofeev, Nikolay. 2019. The I-464 Housing Delivery System: A Tool for Urban Modernisation in the Socialist World and Beyond. *Fabrications* 29 (2): 207–230.

Erofeev, Nikolay, and Łukasz Stanek. 2021. Integrate, Adapt, Collaborate: Comecon Architecture in Socialist Mongolia. *ABE Journal* 19. https://doi.org/10.4000/abe.12362.

Fair, Laura. 2013. Drive-In Socialism: Debating Modernities and Development in Dar Es Salaam, Tanzania. *The American Historical Review* 118 (4): 1077–1104.

Fauveaud, Gabriel. 2020. Reworking the Meanings of Urbanity in Post-Socialist Phnom Penh: Toward a Commodification of Urban Centrality. In *Socialist and Post-Socialist Urbanisms: Critical Reflections from a Global Perspective*, 129–154., Edited by Lisa B. Drummond and Douglas Young. Toronto: University of Toronto Press.

Forbes, Dean K., and Nigel Thrift. 1987. *The Socialist Third World: Urban Development and Territorial Planning*. Oxford: Basil Blackwell.

Folkers, Antoni. 2010. *Modern Architecture in Africa*. Amsterdam: Uitgeverij Boom.

French, Richard Anthony, and F. E. Ian Hamilton. 1979. *The Socialist City: Spatial Structure in Soviet and East European Cities*. New York: Wiley.

Friedman, Jane. 2000. Soviet Mastery of the Skies at the Mayakovsky Metro Station. *Studies in the Decorative Arts* 7 (2): 48–64.

Friedman, Jeremy. 2021. *Ripe for Revolution Building Socialism in the Third World*. Cambridge, MA: Harvard University Press.

Glendinning, Miles. 2009. Cold-War Conciliation: International Architectural Congresses in the late 1950s and early 1960s. *The Journal of Architecture* 14 (2): 197–217.

Grama, Emanuela. 2019. *Socialist Heritage: The Politics of Past and Place in Romania*. Bloomington: Indiana University Press.

Gubkina, Ievgenia. 2016. *Slavutych: Architectural Guide*. Berlin: DOM Publishers.

Harmer, Tanya. 2019. The 'Cuban Question' and the Cold War in Latin America, 1959-1964. *Journal of Cold War Studies* 21 (3): 114–151.

Harris, Steven E. 2013. *Communism on Tomorrow Street: Mass Housing and Everyday Life after Stalin*. Washington, DC: Woodrow Wilson Center Press.

Hirata, Koji. 2023. Mao's Steeltown: Industrial City, Colonial Legacies, and Local Political Economy in Early Communist China. *Journal of Urban History* 49 (1): 85–110.

Hirt, Sonia. 2013. Whatever Happened to the (Post)Socialist City? *Cities* 32 (July): 29–38.

Hirt, Sonia A. 2012. *Iron Curtains: Gates, Suburbs and Privatization of Space in the Post-Socialist City*. Somerset: Wiley.

Hirt, Sonia, and Joseph L. Scarpaci. 2007. Peri-Urban Development in Sofia and Havana: Prospects and Perils in the New Millennium. *Annual Proceedings, The Association for the Study of the Cuban Economy* 17: 288–299.

Hou, Li. 2018. *Building for Oil: Daqing and the Formation of the Chinese Socialist State*. Cambridge, MA: Harvard University Press.

Humphrey, Caroline. 2005. Ideology in Infrastructure: Architecture and Soviet Imagination. *Journal of the Royal Anthropological Institute* 11 (1): 39–58.

Hung, Chang-Tai. 2011. *Mao's New World: Political Culture in the Early People's Republic*. Ithaca: Cornell University Press.

Hung, Wu. 2005. *Remaking Beijing: Tiananmen Square and the Creation of a Political Space*. Chicago: University of Chicago Press.

Iandolo, Alessandro. 2012. The Rise and Fall of the Soviet Model of Development in West Africa, 1957-64. *Cold War History Cold War History* 12 (4): 683–704.

International Union of Architects. 1998. *L'UIA, 1948-1998*. Paris: Epure.

Ivaska, Andrew M. 2002. "Anti-Mini Militants Meet Modern Misses": Urban Style, Gender, and the Politics of "National Culture" in 1960s Dar Es Salaam, Tanzania. *Gender and History* 14 (3): 584–607.

Jenks, Andrew. 2000. A Metro on the Mount: The Underground as a Church of Soviet Civilization. *Technology and Culture* 41 (4): 697–724.

Jovanović, J. 2021. Prefabricating Non-Alignment: The IMS Žeželj System across the Decolonized World. In *History of Construction Cultures*. Edited by João Mascarenhas-Mateus, Ana Paula Pires, Manuel Marques Caiado, and Ivo Veiga, 1st ed., 311–318. London: CRC Press.

Kaganovich, Lazar. 1931. *Socialist Reconstruction of Moscow and Other Cities in the U.S.S.R.* New York: International Publishers.

Kalinovsky, Artemy. 2018. *Laboratory of Socialist Development: Cold War Politics and Decolonization in Soviet Tajikistan*. Ithaca: Cornell University Press.

Kaple, Deborah. 2015. Soviet and Chinese Comrades Look Back at the Friendship Decade. *Modern China Studies* 22 (1): 45–69.

Kiernan, Ben. 2008. *The Pol Pot Regime Race, Power, and Genocide in Cambodia under the Khmer Rouge, 1975-79*. New Haven: Yale University Press.

Kim, Mina, and Inha Jung. 2017. The Planning of Microdistricts in Post-War North Korea: Space, Power, and Everyday Life. *Planning Perspectives* 32 (2): 199–223.

Kotkin, Stephen. 1997. *Magnetic Mountain: Stalinism as a Civilization*. Berkeley: University of California Press.

Kulić, Vladimir. 2017. The Builders of Socialism: Eastern Europe's Cities in Recent Historiography. *Contemporary European History* 26 (3): 545–560.

LaCouture, Elizabeth. 2021. *Dwelling in the World: Family, House, and Home in Tianjin, China, 1860-1960*. New York: Columbia University Press.

Ladd, Brian. 1997. *The Ghosts of Berlin: Confronting German History in the Urban Landscape*. Chicago: University of Chicago Press.

Lebow, Katherine. 2013. *Unfinished Utopia: Nowa Huta, Stalinism, and Polish Society, 1949-56*. Ithaca, NY: Cornell University Press.

Lefebvre, Henri. 1974. *The Production of Space*. London: Wiley-Blackwell.

Li, He, Kevin Lo, and Mark Wang. 2015. Economic Transformation of Mining Cities in Transition Economies: Lessons from Daqing, Northeast China. *International Development Planning Review* 37 (3): 311–328.

Li, Yan. 2014. Building Friendship: Soviet Influence, Socialist Modernity. *Quarterly Journal of Chinese Studies* 2(3): 48–66.

Lokotko, Aleksandr. 2018. *Arkhitektura natsional'naia i arkhitektura fraktal'naia*. Minsk: Izd. Dom "Belorusskaia nauka."

Loomis, John A. 1999. *Revolution of Forms: Cuba's Forgotten Art Schools*. New York: Princeton Architectural Press.

Mark, James, Artemy M. Kalinovsky, and Steffi Marung. 2020. *Alternative Globalizations: Eastern Europe and the Postcolonial World*. Bloomington: Indiana University Press.

Martin, Alexander. 2014. *Enlightened Metropolis: Constructing Imperial Moscow, 1762-1855*. Oxford: Oxford University Press.

McIntyre, Kevin. 1996. Geography as Destiny: Cities, Villages and Khmer Rouge Orientalism. *Comparative Studies in Society and History* 38 (4): 730–758.

Meuser, Philipp, and Dimitrij Zadorin. 2015. *Towards a Typology of Soviet Mass Housing. Prefabrication in the USSR 1955 – 1991*. Berlin: DOM Publishers.

Murawski, Michal. 2018. Actually-Existing Success: Economics, Aesthetics, and the Specificity of (Still-) Socialist Urbanism. *Comparative Studies in Society and History* 60 (4): 907–937.

2019. *The Palace Complex: A Stalinist Skyscraper, Capitalist Warsaw, and a City Transfixed*. Bloomington: Indiana University Press.

Myers, Garth A. 1994. Making the Socialist City of Zanzibar. *Geographical Review* 84 (4): 451–464.

Myers, Garth A. 2003. *Verandahs of Power: Colonialism and Space in Urban Africa*. Syracuse: Syracuse University Press.

Myers, Garth A. 2011. *African Cities: Alternative Visions of Urban Theory and Practice*. London: Bloomsbury Publishing.

Nordlander, David J. 1998. Origins of a Gulag Capital: Magadan and Stalinist Control in the Early 1930s. *Slavic Review* 57 (4): 791–812.

Pan, Yihong. 2002. An Examination of the Goals of the Rustication Program in the People's Republic of China. *Journal of Contemporary China* 11 (31): 361–379.

Patrick Calmon de Carvalho Braga. 2017. Arquitectura Cuba and the Early Revolutionary Project. *International Journal of Cuban Studies* 9 (2): 235–259.

Portnov, Andrii. 2022. *Dnipro: An Entangled History of a European City*. Boston, MA: Academic Studies Press.

Rassweiler, Anne. 1988. *The Generation of Power: The History of Dneprostroi*. Oxford: Oxford University Press.

Reid, Susan. 2009. "Our Kitchen Is Just as Good": Soviet Responses to the American Kitchen. *Cold War Kitchen: Americanization, Technology, and*

European Users, 83–112. Edited by Ruth Oldenziel and Karin Zachmann. Cambridge, MA: MIT Press.

Report from a Conference Organized by the Government of the DPRK on the Issue of Implementing the Plan of Reconstruction for Pyongyang, June 05, 1953, History and Public Policy Program Digital Archive, Polish Foreign Ministry Archive. Obtained for NKIDP by Jakub Poprocki and translated for NKIDP by Maya Latynski. http://digitalarchive.wilsoncenter.org/document/114954.

Rowe, Peter G., and Seng Kuan. 2004. *Architectural Encounters with Essence and Form in Modern China*. Cambridge, MA: MIT Press.

Ruder, Cynthia Ann. 2018. *Building Stalinism: The Moscow Canal and the Creation of Soviet Space*. London: I.B. Tauris.

Ruscitti Harshman, Deirdre. 2018. A Space Called Home: Housing and the Management of the Everyday in Russia, 1890-1935. PhD dissertation, University of Illinois at Urbana-Champaign.

Sammartino, Annemarie. 2018. The New Socialist Man in the *Plattenbau*: The East German Housing Program and the Development of the Socialist Way of Life. *Journal of Urban History* 44 (1): 78–94.

Scarpaci, Joseph L. 2000. Reshaping Habana Vieja: Revitalization, Historic Preservation, and Restructuring in the Socialist City. *Urban Geography* 21 (8): 724–744.

Scarpaci, Joseph L., Roberto Segre, and Mario Coyula. 2002. *Havana: Two Faces of the Antillean Metropolis*. Chapel Hill: University of North Carolina Press.

Schwenkel, Christina. 2014. Spectacular Infrastructure and Its Breakdown in Socialist Vietnam. *American Ethnologist* 42: 520–534.

2015. Reclaiming Rights to the Socialist City: Bureaucratic Artefacts and the Affective Appeal of Petitions. *South East Asia Research* 23 (2): 205–25.

2020. *Building Socialism: The Afterlife of East German Architecture in Urban Vietnam*. Durham: Duke University Press.

2020. From Socialist Moderns to the New Urban Poor: Gender and the Housing Question in Vinh City, Vietnam. In *Socialist and Post-Socialist Urbanisms: Critical Reflections from a Global Perspective*, 27–49. Edited by Lisa B. Drummond and Douglas Young. Toronto: University of Toronto Press.

Segre, Roberto. 2002. *Havana, from Tacón to Forestier. Planning Latin America's Capital Cities, 1850-1950*, 193–213. Edited by Arturo Almandoz. London: Routledge.

Shkvarikov, Viacheslav A. 1967. *Gradostroitel'stvo SSSR 1917-1967*. Moscow: Stroiizdat.

Shin, Gunsoo, and Inha Jung. 2016. Appropriating the Socialist Way of Life: The Emergence of Mass Housing in Post-War North Korea. *The Journal of Architecture* 21 (2): 159–180.

Siddiqi, Asif. 2022. Atomized Urbanism: Secrecy and Security from the Gulag to the Soviet Closed Cities. *Urban History* 49: 190–210.

Slezkine, Yuri. 2019. *House of Government: A Saga of the Russian Revolution*. Princeton: Princeton University Press.

Smith, Mark B. 2010. *Property of Communists: The Urban Housing Program from Stalin to Khrushchev*. DeKalb: Northern Illinois University Press.

Stanek, Łukasz. 2011. *Henri Lefebvre on Space: Architecture, Urban Research, and the Production of Theory*. 1st ed. Minneapolis: University of Minnesota Press.

Stanek, Łukasz. 2012. Introduction: The "Second World's" Architecture and Planning in the "Third World." *The Journal of Architecture* 17 (3): 299–307. https://doi.org/10.1080/13602365.2012.692597.

Stanek, Łukasz. 2020. *Architecture in Global Socialism: Eastern Europe, West Africa and the Middle East in the Cold War*. Princeton: Princeton University Press.

Stanek, Łukasz. 2022. Socialist Worldmaking: The Political Economy of Urban Comparison in the Global Cold War. *Urban Studies* 59 (8): 1575–1596.

Stapleton, Kristin. 2022. *Modern City in Asia*. Cambridge: Cambridge University Press.

Stronski, Paul. 2010. *Tashkent: Forging a Soviet City, 1930-1966*. Pittsburgh: University of Pittsburgh Press.

Swift, Anthony. 1998. The Soviet World of Tomorrow at the New York World's Fair, 1939. *The Russian Review* 57 (3): 364–379.

Taylor, Karin. 2006. *Let's Twist Again: Youth and Leisure in Socialist Bulgaria*. Munster: Lit Verlag.

Trotsky, Leon. 1923. Vodka, the Church, and the Cinema. Pravda. Moscow.

Turner, Fred. 2013. *The Democratic Surround: Multimedia and American Liberalism from World War II to the Psychedelic Sixties*. Chicago: University of Chicago Press.

Tyner, James A., Samuel Henkin, Savina Sirik, and Sokvisal Kimsroy. 2014. Phnom Penh during the Cambodian Genocide: A Case of Selective Urbicide. *Environment and Planning A: Economy and Space* 46 (8): 1873–1891.

van der Straeten, Jonas, and Mariya Petrova. 2022. The Soviet City as a Landscape in the Making: Planning, Building and Appropriating Samarkand, c. 1960s-80s. *Central Asian Survey* 41 (2): 297–321.

van Zon, Hans, Andre Batako, and Anna Kreslavska. 1998. *Social and Economic Change in Eastern Ukraine: The Example of Zaporizhzhya*. Aldershot: Ashgate.

Willimott, Andy. 2017. *Living the Revolution: Urban Communes & Soviet Socialism, 1917-1932*. Oxford: Oxford University Press.

Wimmelbücker, Ludger. 2012. Architecture and City Planning Projects of the German Democratic Republic in Zanzibar. *The Journal of Architecture* 17 (3): 407–432.

Wu, Weiping, and Piper Gaubatz. 2020. *The Chinese City*. Milton: Taylor and Francis.

Young, Glennys. 2011. *The Communist Experience in the Twentieth Century: A Global History through Sources*. Oxford: Oxford University Press.

Zarecor, Kimberly Elman. 2011. *Manufacturing a Socialist Modernity: Housing in Czechoslovakia, 1945-1960*. Pittsburgh: University of Pittsburgh Press.

2018. What Was So Socialist about the Socialist City? Second World Urbanity in Europe. *Journal of Urban History* 44 (1): 95–117.

Zavisca, Jane R. 2012. *Housing the New Russia*. Ithaca: Cornell University Press.

Zubovich, Katherine. 2021. *Moscow Monumental: Soviet Skyscrapers and Urban Life in Stalin's Capital*. Princeton: Princeton University Press.

Acknowledgments

I am grateful to colleagues in the Global Urban History Project and Second World Urbanity group for fostering collaboration and connection across fields and disciplines and for spurring us to think more comparatively and globally. I thank Orysia Kulick and Kristin Stapleton for their generous suggestions on the text. I am grateful also to two anonymous reviewers for their valuable comments. I thank Hareda Fakhrudin for her assistance with early research. Finally, I thank Tracy Neumann for her generous feedback and guidance as I worked on this Element. I also gratefully acknowledge the support of the University at Buffalo College of Arts and Sciences Julian Park Fund, which funded image reproduction and cartography for this Element.

Cambridge Elements

Global Urban History

Michael Goebel

Graduate Institute Geneva

Michael Goebel is the Pierre du Bois Chair Europe and the World and Associate Professor of International History at the Graduate Institute Geneva. His research focuses on the histories of nationalism, of cities, and of migration. He is the author of Anti-Imperial Metropolis: Interwar Paris and the Seeds of Third World Nationalism (2015).

Tracy Neumann

Wayne State University

Tracy Neumann is an Associate Professor of History at Wayne State University. Her research focuses on global and transnational approaches to cities and the built environment. She is the author of Remaking the Rust Belt: The Postindustrial Transformation of North America (2016) and of essays on urban history and public policy.

Joseph Ben Prestel

Freie Universität Berlin

Joseph Ben Prestel is an Assistant Professor (wissenschaftlicher Mitarbeiter) of history at Freie Universität Berlin. His research focuses on the histories of Europe and the Middle East in the nineteenth and twentieth centuries as well as on global and urban history. He is the author of Emotional Cities: Debates on Urban Change in Berlin and Cairo, 1860–1910 (2017).

About the Series

This series proposes a new understanding of urban history by reinterpreting the history of the world's cities. While urban history has tended to produce single-city case studies, global history has mostly been concerned with the interconnectedness of the world. Combining these two approaches produces a new framework to think about the urban past. The individual titles in the series emphasize global, comparative, and transnational approaches. They deliver empirical research about specific cities, while also exploring questions that expand the narrative outside the immediate locale to give insights into global trends and conceptual debates. Authored by established and emerging scholars whose work represents the most exciting new directions in urban history, this series makes pioneering research accessible to specialists and non-specialists alike.

Cambridge Elements

Global Urban History

Elements in the Series

How Cities Matter
Richard Harris

Real Estate and Global Urban History
Alexia Yates

Cities and News
Lila Caimari

The Modern City in Asia
Kristin Stapleton

Epidemic Cities
Antonio Carbone

Urban Disasters
Cindy Ermus

Making Cities Socialist
Katherine Zubovich

A full series listing is available at: www.cambridge.org/EGUB.

For EU product safety concerns, contact us at Calle de José Abascal, 56–1°,
28003 Madrid, Spain or eugpsr@cambridge.org.

www.ingramcontent.com/pod-product-compliance
Ingram Content Group UK Ltd.
Pitfield, Milton Keynes, MK11 3LW, UK
UKHW022146080726
473066UK00010B/786

* 9 7 8 1 1 0 8 7 9 7 1 0 8 *